THE BIG BOOK OF APPS

Your Nerdy BFF's Guide to
(Almost) Every App in the Universe

THE BIG BOOK OF APPS

Your Nerdy BFF's Guide to (Almost) Every App in the Universe

by Beth Ziesenis
Your Nerdy Best Friend

The Big Book of Apps

Your Nerdy BFF's Guide to (Almost) Every App in the Universe

Library of Congress Control Number:

ISBN-13: 978-0692924785
ISBN-10: 0692924787

Printed in the United States of America

Your Nerdy Best Friend Ink
5694 Mission Center Road, Suite 602-111
San Diego, CA 92108
yournerdybestfriend.com

One of the joys of being a speaker happens between sessions
when proud parents approach me to brag about
their little nerds at home.
They say…

My daughter is a nerd, and all her friends think she's cool.
My son is 8 and learning to code.
My niece just got glasses and wears them with pride.

I'm so happy to hear about these kids
who have found their places in the world
and are embracing their differences.

Dedicated to the world's little nerds
(especially my nephews, Jamison and Ashton)…
the children who will soon lead us
into new technology frontiers.

Acknowledgements

Shout Outs

The NerdHerd members (Page xvii) are my heroes because they believed in the book so much that they pre-ordered it. But they're not the only people who deserve my thanks...

- She who figured out where all the little nerd cartoons would go:
  Designer Marian Hartsough

- She who kept my business going while I focused on the book:
  Manager Molly Gardner

- He who designed the cover:
  Designer Sherwin Soy

- He who puts up with me:
  Husband D.J. Rausa

Overly Honest Reviews of Beth Z and Her Books

• •

This random collection of quotes about yours truly and *The Big Book of Apps* includes…

- Famous people I hope will impress you
- My Nerdy Best Friends (other tech experts)
- People who have hired me to speak
- Friends and family I cajoled into writing endorsements
- My long-suffering husband

Arguably the Most Famous Guy in This List

Beth understands that craftspeople are only as good as their tools. And these are the new tools, the tools for a new generation of work.

> **THE Seth Godin**
> Author, *Lynchpin: Are You Indispensable?*
>   and a whole bunch of other books
> sethgodin.com

A Famous Guy on the Radio Who Made an App

I Love Beth Z... well I don't know her well enough to say I LOVE her, but I sure like her a lot... well... I haven't spent enough time to say I LIKE her, but I've seen her around the halls of the National Speakers Association convention and I hear she's great.

Beth heard that I'm kind of a big deal because I'm on the SiriusXM Radio Family Comedy Channels, and she thought it might help her book if I endorsed it. I told her I'd consider it if she endorsed my new app, You're Done (Page 119), which allows you to lock your kids' phone at the push of a button.

Beth's book is in my bathroom and I read it every chance I get. It's awesome!

> **Patrick Henry**
> Entertainer and Author
> patrickhenryspeaker.com

My Husband

As Beth's husband, I'd like to personally thank you for buying The Big Book of Apps. *We have about 400,000 more copies in the garage, and I'm hoping she sells enough so I can store my bikes.*

> **D.J. Rausa**
> Student Loan Lawyer and Beth's Long-Suffering Husband
> debtdoc.com

A Guy Who Is on TV News a Lot

Let's be honest—do you really know what an APP is? Sure, you have them on your phone and you download whichever ones your teenager or your niece tells you are awesome... but do you really understand them? I know I don't. Lucky for us both we know Beth Ziesenis. And Beth not only understands apps but she knows which ones work and which ones you should use. Best part of Beth's The Big Book of Apps? *You don't have to understand them—you just have to listen to Beth!*

> **Bruce Turkel**
> Speaker and Author
> bruceturkel.com

The First Viral YouTube Video Guy

Is there anything that changes faster than the world of apps? All things evolve… I should know. I created "The Evolution of Dance," once the most watched video on YouTube (but then Justin Bieber hit puberty and some guy named Psy taught us Gangnam Style).

Since things are always changing, it's good to have someone who can help you navigate. And when it comes to the world of apps, Beth, Your Nerdy BFF, does just that! Her book is a great clear breakdown of all things apps!

> **Judson Laipply**
> Inspirational Comedian, World's First YouTube Celebrity
>   and Creator of "The Evolution of Dance"
> judsonlaipply.com

A Group that Bought a Bunch of Books for Companies that Sell Forklifts

Our organization purchased over 600 of Beth's books to provide our members with a valuable and practical resource. Beth has a knack for breaking down technology, social media and apps into user friendly and easy-to-understand small bytes (pun intended). She has presented workshops to our association members several times, and the takeaway value is tremendous. We are looking forward to reading her latest masterpiece!

> **Liz Richards**
> CEO, Materials Handling Equipment Distributors Association
> mheda.org

A Nerdy BFF

Beth Z has done it again! If you want to get past what apps are "new and shiny" to those that are actually helpful in real life, this is the book for you! Written in an easy-to-follow format, our Nerdy Best Friend has made apps accessible to the masses!

> **Crystal Washington, CSP**
> Futurist and Technology Strategist
> crystalwashington.com

Another Nerdy BFF

Do you know every app you could possibly use to be more productive and more profitable? I bet you don't. But if you buy The Big Book of Apps, *you'll know all the best ones—with creative tips on how to use them. The time you save with just one section will make this book practically free—and if you don't find at least 10 apps you didn't know about, you're a bigger geek than me.*

Phil Gerbyshak
Chief Digital Officer
Vengreso.com

A BFF Who Is TOTALLY Not a Tech Nerd

I'm not a nerd. I'm a dork. I do not do the technologies. I am still navigating learning how to work televisions that use "remote controls." Beth bridges this gap with her clear understanding that I (and you) need help and help is out there and even possibly in my own pocket devices. Who knew? Beth does!

Jessica Pettitt
Speaker, Author and Luddite
goodenoughnow.com

My Dad

As Beth's father, I am responsible for her great storehouse of knowledge and quick wit. I bought the first computer for the family, a Commodore VIC-20. Early the next morning, I woke to hear our new computer beeping as she carefully typed one of the programs that came with the computer. We even produced and programmed our own game.

The VIC-20 came with no apps. I explained to Beth that these toy computers would never catch on. I told her the mainframe was the only computer you need to learn how to use and that she should learn to program because all these apps would never help her make a living.

Now she is an internationally known author and lecturer who specializes in apps, and I am looking for a mainframe to program.

So buy this book... her father needs some money.

Scott Ziesenis
Retired Programmer and Papa

My Sister

Beth was always a nerd. It's nice that she gets paid for it now. I just hope that someday she'll finally get an invitation to a prom.

Sarah Ziesenis
High-School Science Teacher and Baby Sister

A Super Speaker Friend (And a Really Smart Chick)

The Big Book of Apps *cuts through the thousands of apps and tells you which ones you really need to consider to make your life better. Save time and frustration by getting this book and doing what Beth says!*

Mary C. Kelly, Ph.D., CSP
Author, *Why Leaders Fail* and *The 7 Prescriptions for Success*
productiveleaders.com

The Only Guy I Know Who Kinda Ran for President

I have too many apps already on my devices. But how do I cut them down? How do I know which ones I really need? Easy enough, I go to the go-to on this—the same expert who taught me how to make images a few years back so my social media posts rocked. The one and only Beth Ziesenis. I'm so glad she has a new book on this because I trust her judgment and recommendations completely.

Dave Lieber, CSP
Watchdog Columnist at *The Dallas Morning News*
dallasnews.com/news/watchdog

I Owe This Chick a Drink

In the hundreds of interviews I've done over the years for the Association Chat podcast, Beth Z. has been one of the most talked about. People love Beth Z., and it's easy to see why! After listening to her for a few minutes you'll hear about an app that will change your business, and by the time you've talked with her for an hour, she will have introduced some technology that will change your life! The Big Book of Apps *is a lifesaver for the time-strapped executive who needs to know which tech tools to install to rule the world from her smartphone!*

By the way… Beth Z. still owes me a cocktail when I see her at the next conference. I have a cool reminder app she suggested to me once that tells me so.

KiKi L'Italien
CEO, Amplified Growth and Association Chat
amplifiedgrowth.net
associationchat.com

A Famous Author Who Has Been on Oprah and Donahue (and Who Leno Joked About in a Monologue)

Beth Ziesenis really IS my Nerdy Best Friend. No, I mean that. Literally. She has taken the place of my former nerdy best friend, Sheldon Cooper. And even though THOUSANDS of people already consider Beth to be THEIR Nerdy Best Friend, I'm certain she has room for you, too.

Greg Godek
Author, *1001 Ways to Be Romantic*
　　and *How to be Mildly Brilliant*
theahhacompany.com

A Guy Who Knew Me Way Back When

Before Beth Z started writing books, I caught one of her presentations at a conference. My first thought was, "If this nerd polishes up her presentation style, she'll be a force to be reckoned with."

Here we are years later, and Beth is still not very polished, speaker-wise. But that's because she's not a speaker—she's truly our Nerdy Best Friend! And she just gets up there and shares her brilliance with nerdy passion. So who cares about the polish?!

She has always been my go-to resource and TRUSTED advisor for app recommendations. Now, in her fourth powerful book, she's got virtually everything I could need! I fear I won't have to email her ever again. (But of course I will—because she's also delightful!)

Gary Rifkin
Chief Learning Officer, CoreClarity, Inc.
coreclarity.net

The First Guy Who Hired Me to Write

Beth Ziesenis makes your phone so useful your laptop will be jealous.

I write computer books for a living, but I'm embarrassed to admit that before reading Beth's books, my knowledge of apps ranked somewhere between Your Grandparents Who Still Have a VCR and Dude Who Just Discovered Angry Birds.

Now that I've read The Big Book of Apps, *when I converse with the youth of today, I'm not just yelling at them to get off my lawn. We talk about cool new apps. Then I tell them to get off my lawn.*

There are great apps all over these pages, but I'm a particular fan of RunPee, Page 146. I never dreamed I'd live in an age when my phone told me when to pee so I didn't miss an integral plot point of Kung Fu Panda 3.

Rogers Cadenhead
Author, *Sams Teach Yourself Java in 24 Hours*
java24hours.com

The World's First Neurohumorist (So She Knows Funny)

Beth Z not only KNOWS her stuff, she knows how to PRESENT her stuff! There are lots of techie experts out there, but none of them present their knowledge—in print AND on stage–with the wit and depth that Beth does.

Karyn Buxman
Neurohumorist
karynbuxman.com

The Person I Pay to Like Me (My Manager)

The Big Book of Apps *is the* Moby Dick *of technology books. And Beth Z is the Hemingway of Nerds. I keep all four of Beth's books on my desk… my desk at the Nerdy Best Friend office… where I get paid… by Beth.*

But, honestly, this book is a classic and the tools in it will change the way you run your business and manage your team. Every one of these apps is nerd-tested and geek-approved. Enjoy!

Private note to Beth: Is this what you wanted me to say?

Molly Gardner
Manager, Your Nerdy Best Friend
yournerdybestfriend.com

Legacy NerdHerders

The NerdHerd members are people who pre-purchased this book—and in some cases the other ones! Look for the NerdHerd Approved badge to see their app recommendations.

These wonderful supporters have been members of the NerdHerd from the beginning.

American Mensa

Beth Bridges, The Networking Motivator

Beth Surmont

Carol Campbell

Chris Lyles

Debbi Babashanian

Debbie Lowenthal

Denise M. Smith

Don Pendley

Emily Arrowsmith

Gary Rifkin

Gianna Caruso

Gina Sutherland

Jamison & Ashton Barcelona

Jeffrey A. Horn

Jerry Huffman

Joanne St-Pierre

Kathleen Wilson

Kim Williams

Kimberly Lilley

Lindsey Haley

Loretta Peskin

Melissa Heeke

Michele Huber

Nancy McCulley

Nora Y. Onishi

Roki Vargas

Scott Ziesenis, aka Papa

Terry Murphy

Tesha Hoff

Tina Baldwin

Tom Wright

Two-Time NerdHerders

Thanks to the people who have supported two of the nerdy books.

Barbara ER Lucas

Big Papa Von Kaenel

Billie Jean Turner

Carol Lane

Cheryl Bowie, CTA & Owner, In-Joy Travel

Cheryl Paglia

Chris Champion

Clark Jones

Cory Davis

dawnsy designs

Di Richards

Diane Hohnstein

Eileen Blake

Francine Butler

Gloria Rossiter

Heather Rae Osborne

Jan Leighton

Johanne Stogran

John Zink

Karen Holt Peterson

Kathleen M. Fitzpatrick

Kerri S. Wilson

Linda Whale de Vargas

Lisa Prats

Lowell Aplebaum

Margaret Maes

Marlene LaMoure Urbach, R.N., MBA

Mary C. Kelly, Ph.D., CSP

Monica J. McCorkle

Nanci McMaken

Patricia Wright

Phil Gerbyshak

Renae Hinchey

Rita Tayenaka

Shannon Carroll

Shawn Powelson

Steven Jones

Stuart Sweeney

Tami DuBose

Tim & Shana Teehan

Tracy Taraski

Vickie Lester

Welcome to the NerdHerd

● ●

These supporters joined the NerdHerd so they could be in *The Big Book of Apps!*

Alan Shark

Allyson Pahmer

Alma Roman

Alyssa Godfrey

Andrea Wilson

Andrew Hartman

Ann Blackman

Ann Dahlke

Anne Curcurito

APH

Austin Fonda

Barbara Hamilton

Bernadette Patton

Bert Hultman

Bill Dent

Bill Grubb

Bill Soellner

Bob Eichhorn

Brad Anderson

Camille White, COPM

Candy Joyce

Carolyn House

Carolyn Parkin

Carolyn Rauch

Cecelia Peabody

Celia Fritz-Watson

Charles Ottman

Cheryl Eastbourne

Cheryl Locke

Chris Christensen

Chris Eisenberg

Chris Legge

Cindy Camargo

Cindy Cara

Colette Collier Trohan

Craig Borner

Crissy Hancock

Cynthia S. Philbrook

Darcy Burnett

Darla Nickens Hunley

David Giger

David Littleton

Deann McKeever

Debbie Whalen

Deborah Brandt

Debra Mandala

Deidre Schexnayder

Denny Vincent

Diana Hersch

Dilip Divecha

Donna Mikesh

Donna Mortensen, CAP-OM

Donna Olewinski

Donna Taylor

Doris Nurenberg

Dorothy Kryskowski

Dr. Juan Lorenzo Martinez Colon

Duane Washkowiak

Elizabeth Bartz

Elizabeth Calamito

Elizabeth Cogan

Ellen Wodiuk

Ellie Taylor

Emily Garner

Fran Rickenbach

Frank Lessing

Garry Wicker

Gay Wilson

Gerry McEvoy

Gina Jones

Ginger Luby

Glenn Panner

Gregory J. Paveza

Hayley Gunther

Heather Hill

Helen Luna Fess R.

Jim Neyer

James B. Martin

Jamie Rice

Jamie Uphold

Janelle Zamora

Janet Mahoney-Hubert

Jason Burton

Jeanee Gilson

Jennifer LeBlanc

Jennifer OLeary

Jeremy Shugars

Jill Tamborini

Jim Petersen

Joanne Olson

Jody Shelton Stephen

John Coen

John Craighill

John DeWyer

John Silwonuk

Johnna Mills

Jonathan Gorman

Joyce Pleva

Joyce R. Nakamura

Judie Docs

Judy Rhodes

Julie Lynch

Julie Mills

Julie Perrine, Founder & CEO, All Things Admin

Karen Evangelisti

Karen Farley

Karen Tilson

Karlene Dittrich

Karyn Buxman & Greg Godek

Kasey Nored

Kathy Dunn

Kaye Lewis

Kelley Geyer

Kelley Pitts

Kimberly Haase

Kitty Collins

Kristi Elizondo

Kristin Clarke

Kristine R. Nelson

Laura McConnell

Laura Young

Linda Dagostino

Linda Gobler

Linda Raynes

Linda Siy

Lisa Braithwaite, Public Speaking Coach and Trainer

Lisa Gurske

Lisa Macdonald

Lisa Priepot

Lois Creamer

Loretta Mingram

Lori Palermo & Dave Brow

Lucinda Harrison-Cox

Lucy Bottorff

Lydia Rouzeau

Lynette Pendergast

Lynn Ferren

Lynn Lockwood

Maggie Harris

Maggie Morris

Malcolm Sweet

Marcia Clarke

Marianne McCreary

Mark Coby

Mary J. Surina

Mary Nelson

Melissa Hull

Melissa Malechek

Michele Rackey

Michelle Grachek

Micki Novak

Mike Hayes

Miles & Panda

Nancy Sharp

Nancy Cooper Upchurch, CAP-OM

Nancy Vicuna

Nicole French

Nicole Toombs

Noel Hoekstra

Norma Castrejon

Norman Harvey

Pam Bradley

Pam Cochran

Pam Stanley

Pamela Lewis

Patricia McFadden

Piedmont Regional AOR Member

Shelley Graves, Purple Passion
     Media

Rachael Alter

Rae Lathrop

Raven, the Internal Audit Trainer

Reinette Carrico

Rich Schwartz

Richard Wright

Robin Sagadraca

Roger Nelson

Ronni Maestas

Roxanne Daiuto

SA SCUBA Shack

Sam Richter

Sandy Baker

Scott Childs

Scott Davis

Shawna Suckow

Shelley Paik

Sherrie & Mark Rosenberger

Sheryl Buckner

Sheryll Dahlke

Shirley Meine

Sondra Goodman

Steph Buell

Steven Keeley

Superior Office Support, LLC

Susan Armbrester

Susan Difani

Susan Moss

Susan Motley

Susan Sokolowsky

Susan Wainwright

Sydney Isaac

Sylvia Ayers

Team Dynamics LLC

Terri DeFlorian

Tim Zielenbach

Timothy Burch

Todd Fleischer

Tracy Eades

Valerie Zelmer

Valinda & Bill Lessin

Vesta Smith

Vicki Glardon

Vikki Mitchell

Table of Contents

Security Tools 117

Personal Growth and Career   179

Health 201

Wake Up in Style 202

Get Active 204

Watch What I Eat 207

Stay Calm 210

Step Away from the Computer 214

Stay Healthy 217

Design   241

How to Use This Book

· ·

Dear Readers,

This book is a guide to (almost) every app in the universe—or at least more than 450 of them. My hope is that you read my books and leave my sessions with the idea that the tech world is full of amazing tools that you can start using right away. Maybe you start using Zoom (Page 42) for your videoconferences but then you realize you need something more and search around to see what is out there. My recommendations should open your eyes to a mindboggling world of technology you never knew existed.

When you read this book, keep these thoughts in mind:

This Book Is a Starting Point

The Big Book of Apps is organized by questions that you may ask and the apps that answer those questions. For each question, you'll find a couple of main recommendations plus several alternates. But the questions and the tools that answer them are by no means exhaustive. My goal is to get you started in the right direction so you can find what you need.

These Tools Are Awesome

I chose these particular tools for their dependability, multiplatform availability, popularity and ease of use. If you've attended any of my presentations, this book serves as the missing manual for many of the tools I talk about.

These Tools Are a Starting Point

For the most part, each tool is just one option in a very crowded and competitive category. I included alternatives to each, but that list is just a starting place for a plethora of competitors.

This Book Is Out of Date

We triple checked the pricing, platforms and functionality of the tools in this book right up until we pushed the print button, but the next week, the descriptions will be out of date. The good news is that most of the changes you'll see will probably be growth in availability and functionality—unless Microsoft eats it. Then the tool is gone.

Look for changes in these areas:

- Platform availability (access via new operating systems, etc.)
- Pricing (up and down)
- Extra-special features (groundbreaking, oh-my-gosh functionality with big announcements)
- Integrations and partnerships (increasing every day)
- Incorporation into "The Internet of Things," like IFTTT (Page 156) logging how many times your smart dishwasher runs or Evernote (Page 22) automatically sending new recipes to your smart stove

Despite these inevitable changes and advancements, you can be confident that this book will serve as the starting place for putting this technology into action for your work, home and life.

Organize

· ·

I want to . . .

Manage Schedules

••

I bet that zero people reading this book can keep track of every commitment they have at every moment of every day. We all need calendars—and more—we all need calendars that we can see and update from any device at any time.

Start with...

Google Calendar

The Calendar to Rule Them All

google.com/calendar

Google Calendar is a free tool to create and share multiple calendars and import other calendar feeds so your whole schedule is available when and where you need it.

Few tools offer as much versatility as Google Calendar. You might consider it the building block of your time management system. The beauty of this relatively simple tool is its ability to import from, export to and integrate with an ever-increasing mountain of other apps and systems.

NerdHerder Hayley Gunther likes the way Google Calendar gives her one view of her schedule. "I have 5 different email accounts for 5 different jobs. I have one calendar to enter all of the appointments, including non-Gmail accounts. It emails my primary account a daily agenda at 5 AM every day. I would be lost without it."

Then Try...

Fantastical 2 (iOS)

Best Apple Calendar App
flexibits.com

Because of the death of my favorite calendar app, Sunrise, or rather its absorption into Microsoft's products, I've migrated to **Fantastical 2** for my iOS calendar needs. As expected, Fantastical lets you use your Google Calendar as the basis for the tools. It also can integrate into your contacts and Apple reminders to help you remember birthdays, plus Apple reminders to help, well, remind you of stuff. True Apple fan? Use the touch feature on newer Apple devices for a sneak peek at your calendar, and add in apps for your Mac and Apple Watch.

CloudCal (Android)

Because Fantastical Doesn't Have an Android Version
pselis.com

CloudCal not only integrates with Google—it also lets you pull in Microsoft products such as Outlook and Exchange. Another unique feature is CloudCal's Magic Circles that display the day's meetings on a round clock face.

Also Check Out...

Jorte

Multi-Platform Calendar No One Has Heard Of
jorte.com

I've heard wonderful things about **Jorte**, but I bet you haven't. Of the millions of downloads, almost a third have been from Japan. Jorte synchronizes with calendars like the others, but its biggest feature is the cross-platform capability: Windows, Android and Apple.

NerdHerd Thumbs Up: Track Your Time

Toggl
Time-Tracking Tool for Clients and Projects
toggl.com

My NerdHerd buddy Beth Bridges uses **Toggl** to track the time she spends on individual projects and client work. "It's very quick and easy to set up, simple to use… and yet powerful to track time spent and increasing productivity."

Manage Family Schedules and Projects

As a working adult, you need to track tasks, keep in touch with team-mates, manage inventory and schedule meetings and events. What about your duties at home? Running a household isn't all that different from running a business.

Start with...

Cozi
Family-Friendly Calendar Manager
cozi.com

Year after year, parents in my audiences tell me the best calendar tool is **Cozi Family Organizer**. Cozi lets you set up calendars for each family member and combines them on your master calendar. You can also import other calendars, such as soccer and school schedules. The system also includes family-oriented lists to help with shopping, chores and more. Google Calendar (Page 2) can bring together the same types of family calendars, complete with color coding and notifications, but Cozi adds the convenient tools that make it perfect for family management.

NerdHerders Susan Sokolowsky and Steven Keeley both list Cozi as a favorite. Susan likes that the whole family can access the shopping list, and Steven says, "I don't have to send emails or track people down to see if they are available. It all syncs in one place."

Then Try...

Grocery iQ
Cloud-Based Grocery Lists
groceryiq.com

Grocery iQ is another suggestion from audience members. Create a grocery list online or via the apps, and you can see it and share it on any device. The system uses predictive text to help you quickly create your lists and lets you add items by scanning UPC codes and adding things from your history.

One cool feature is the app's ability to organize your list by grocery store aisle, so no more zigzagging from produce to pet foods and back again. Another bonus: The service comes from Coupons.com, so you can find and print money-saving offers for your lists.

Also Check Out...

Out of Milk
Home-Centered To-Do List Tool
outofmilk.com

NerdHerder Sydney Isaac loves **Out of Milk**, a task list tool that works well for grocery lists. "I don't have to write my list each and every time I need to do something, especially if I have done it before. Out of Milk remembers. I can add things on the fly because I always have my list with me!"

Manage Lists

●●

My secret shame: my "high-tech" task list manager is a pen and a spiral-bound notebook. I can't use an electronic list maker because I'm too easily distracted online. I have to have a physical list in front of me and the absolute joy of crossing things off.

Start with...

Todoist
My Manager's Favorite Productivity Tool
todoist.com

NerdHerd
approved

I'm putting **Todoist** at the top of my list of list tools based on the masterful way my business manager uses it to keep Nerd HQ on track. Molly Gardner uses Todoist for every part of her life, from our short-term projects to our long-term ideas to the home projects she'll get to someday.

Like many of the top task list tools, Todoist lets you sync your lists on any device. When Molly forces me to use it, I find the integration with Gmail (Page 64) very helpful, because I can turn emails into tasks and throw them back on her plate with a couple of clicks. I never needed more than the free version, but Molly finds the extra features in premium very helpful, such as more projects, location-based reminders and the capability to work with more collaborators.

Todoist gets extra points for its natural-language task skills (such as "remind me to make my car payment on the first of every month starting in October"), as well as its integrations with IFTTT (Page 156) and Zapier (Page 157).

Molly's not the only one who loves Todoist. NerdHerder Dawn James says, "This to-do list attaches to Outlook, allows you to prioritize and group items by project, and (if you pay) attach notes, documents and links to the items on the list. Plus, as you check items off of the list, you earn Todoist Karma points! Who doesn't love to earn points?"

Then Try...

I'm hard pressed to name significant differences among the top task list services. You'll find ways to make lists, organize lists, search lists, share lists and, most importantly, cross things off the lists. Here are a few bullet points to explore regarding some of the bigger tools, but the best idea is to download several and give them a try.

Microsoft To-Do

The App that Ate Award-Winning Wunderlist

todo.microsoft.com

Wunderlist has been around for years and has garnered awards and accolades. Microsoft released **To-Do** in the spring of 2017, absorbing the older tool, which it had purchased in 2014. And people are sad. The new app should have the best characteristics of Wunderlist, but people are still sad.

Wunderlist fans are still waiting for Microsoft To-Do to bring all the features to the new app. But here's a list of NerdHerders who mourn the death of Wunderlist and why they loved the app. Notice how all of them used exclamation points to prove their enthusiasm!

Gary Rifkin	Wunderlist helps me stay organized and get things done! In addition to the typical "to-do list" feature, I LOVE how easy it is to share lists and work them with collaborators. It's fully featured and extremely intuitive. It's my MUST HAVE app!
Missy Malechek	Wunderlist makes my chaotic life wonderful! My many lists are never lost and are exactly the same on phone, tablet and desktop!
Crissy Hancock	It keeps me organized across all platforms. I don't have to continually search for my list… it's always at my fingertips. I can share the lists and delegate tasks, and it's all in one place!
Deann McKeever	You can easily see what you have going on and set reminders for anything that may be pressing. Great for organization!

Any.do
Simple Task Manager with Day-by-Day Manager
any.do

People adore **Any.do** for its simplicity. I'm fond of the day planner feature that helps you prioritize the day's events. You can also use the gamification incentives with Any.do to make task management fun (kidding—to-do lists are not fun).

WorkFlowy
Insanely Simple Task Management Tool
workflowy.com

Compared with the beauty and features of the other top apps, **WorkFlowy** is just plain boring. It looks like an outline on a piece of paper. It's not for me, but millions of people adore it.

Also Check Out...

Any List
A NerdHerder's Favorite Task Management App
anylistapp.com

Legacy NerdHerder Melissa Heeke likes **Any List**. "This app helps me to stay organized by creating to-do lists, to-buy lists (groceries!), etc., and to collaborate on lists online and via the app. Very handy!"

Backup Computer and Files

• •

Although cloud storage services do keep a copy of your files on their servers, experts say you shouldn't rely on them as your backup system. I use a couple of external hard drives as well as duplicate data on both Dropbox (Page 14) and Google Drive (Page 15) to back up everything I own. This system has saved my butt more than once—including the time my computer started smoking right before a presentation, and I had to buy a brand new machine for another engagement the very next day. #justifiablyparanoid

Start with...

CrashPlan
The Backup-with-a-Buddy Plan
code42.com/crashplan

IDrive
Backup Service with Extended Archiving
idrive.com

When using online backup services, you generally set up an account; tell them which drives, folders and files to back up; and let them get to work. They can work in the background all the time or back up on a schedule. If your computer blows up, you can restore your files or even every bit and byte of your computer to another machine or recover an earlier version of your files.

If I didn't use hard drives, I'd choose **CrashPlan**. The free version, aptly named CrashPlan Free, puts the backup network into your hands by allowing you to connect to friends' computers for storage. You back up to someone else's computer while he stores his backup on yours. Neither one of you can see the other's files, but everyone has peace of mind—without a monthly subscription fee. The paid versions start at $60 per year.

IDrive receives a big thumbs up from *PC Magazine* for its reasonable prices (about the same money as CrashPlan but for more devices), unlimited archiving and other super-extra features.

Then Try...

SOS Online Backup
Super-Fast Backup Service with Unlimited Version Archiving
sosonlinebackup.com

SOS gets great reviews as well and has the added feature of being incredibly fast in comparison to the other services.

Also Check Out...

Digi.me
Social Media Account Backups
digi.me

Frostbox
Social Media Account Backups Plus Gmail and Evernote
frostbox.com

Are your tweets and Facebook posts works of art? **Digi.me** and **Frostbox** can help you preserve them forever so your kids and grand-kids have a permanent record of what you ate for breakfast every day and your reviews of local cupcake shops.

When I first heard about these tools, I thought it was a nutty idea. Why would you need to keep a copy of your Facebook posts? And who wants to keep all the old tweets? But some high-profile hacks in the past couple of years brought all kinds of important questions into play. If Facebook fails, what happens to all the awesome photo albums you've created? And how can you get back all your Gmail (Page 64) contacts if the service blows up one day?

Both back up the data from social media sites such as Twitter, Facebook and Instagram. Frostbox also includes Gmail and Evernote (Page 22), which may justify the $70 per year price, which is 10 times the cost of Digi.me.

Organize and Store Files

Cloud storage systems have been around for years. They've proven themselves to be an essential business tool for many professionals.

Even though many of the leading tools offer the same types of services, you'll find small differences that may affect how you choose to use them.

Common Characteristics of Cloud Storage Systems

The cloud storage service field is very, very crowded; but a handful of companies lead the pack. In a nutshell, they serve as your hard drive—everywhere. When you sign up for an account, you download the software to your machine and install apps on your devices. The system creates a folder on your computer, and anything you place into that folder is available anywhere you need it.

Most of the major players in this field have many of the same characteristics and capabilities. Here's a summary of the features you'll find in most (if not all) of the top tools.

- Free storage of 2–16GB, including the capability to earn more when you spread the word
- Web and mobile apps to access your files from anywhere
- Real-time synchronization wherever the service is installed
- Two-factor authentication options for enhanced security
- Secure, encrypted storage with strong security measures to protect your files
- Capability to restore deleted files and older versions
- Collaboration via shared folders or files, sometimes with different levels of permissions
- Instant file and folder sharing via links
- Integration with third-party apps for enhanced features and accessibility

Start with...

Dropbox
Arguably the Best Cloud Storage System
dropbox.com

Dropbox is perhaps the most well-known tool in this category, and it boasts the most third-party integrations. Dropbox gives 2GB of storage for free, and you can earn up to 16GB by inviting colleagues and through other tasks. Paid versions start at less than $10 a month for 1TB of storage, which is a helluva lot.

Dropbox is known for personal accounts—they're working on growing the business side. You can collaborate via Paper tool plus inside Microsoft Office 365. On a higher paid version, the Smart Sync option makes access to files not stored on your hard drive a lot faster. Otherwise the synchronization can be kinda slow.

Then Try...

Box
Business-Focused Cloud Storage System
box.com

Box is focusing almost exclusively on the business market. For the personal level, Box gives you 10GB with the free plan, but you'll have to pay extra for version tracking and some of the other features Dropbox gives for free. Starting at $5 per user on the business plans, you can start collaborating (but just between paid users). For $15 per user per month, you can enable project management with tasks and deadlines.

A cool feature with Box is the built-in editing software. Box has its own software that lets you edit and create documents within the system, as well as through outside software such as Microsoft Office and Google.

Google Drive

Google's Cloud Storage System
google.com/drive

Google Drive gives you 15GB free plus unlimited photo and video storage through Google Photos (Page 19), though your storage is shared between your regular files as well as Gmail (Page 64) messages and attachments. 100GB will cost you just $24 a year. As one might expect, Google Drive integrates seamlessly with all things Google. You also have built-in software for editing and creating.

One of Google Drive's coolest features is the real-time collaboration. If you have several committee members working on the same document at the same time, their words and changes appear on the screen, color-coded and even labeled with the users' names. Like Dropbox, Google Drive gives you the ability to revert to older versions of files.

Another great characteristic of Google Drive is its multimedia sharing capabilities, which make it easier to watch video online without having to download.

I often ask my Fancy Hands assistants (Page 160) to use a Google Sheet to collect data, and sometimes I type them little messages while they're working away to freak them out. It's one of my small nerdy joys.

Bonus! In 2017, Google added a **Backup and Sync** tool to help you, well, backup and sync. It's an easier process than the Google Drive app used to require to keep secure copies of your files and photos.

Microsoft OneDrive

Microsoft's Cloud Storage System
onedrive.com

OneDrive's primary purpose is to make it easy to store Microsoft documents when you have a Microsoft 365 subscription. Although anyone can get an account with 15GB of free storage or 50GB starting at $1.99 per month, if you're a subscriber, you get 1TB free.

OneDrive lets users communicate in real time when they're in Microsoft Office documents. At least that's what the website says. I did experiments with a number of contributors but never really got it to work (but I'm a lonely nerd who works alone most of the time). The collaboration mostly takes place through the web app, and it wasn't really convenient for anyone.

Amazon Drive

Amazon's Cloud Storage System
amazon.com/clouddrive

Amazon is responsible for some serious computing power behind the scenes. Not only do many internet entities store their sites and data on Amazon servers, but the giant company also offers cloud storage to normal people like you and me.

Amazon Drive is definitely more of a personal storage solution than a tool you'd use for work, although you can still share files from the drive. You get 5GB free plus unlimited storage for photos if you're a member of Amazon Prime. Unlike Google Photos (Page 19), Amazon lets you upload the photos in full resolution but limits your video uploads to 5GB. Like Google Drive, Amazon Drive is great for watching movies from your media collection.

Also Check Out...

Findo

Search Tool for Multiple Cloud Services
findo.com

If you've ever spent time cursing at the computer as you try to track down the location of a file ("Did I store the dang thing in Dropbox or Google Drive??"), you may enjoy **Findo**. This app lets you link to multiple cloud services such as Dropbox, Box (Page 14), Google Drive (Page 15) and Gmail (Page 64). Then you can search in one place to find your files. Findo also works with natural language, so you can ask it to find the document from the Chicago office that someone sent last month.

Hot Topic:
Are My Files Safe in the Cloud?

You may be reluctant to store files in the cloud because of concerns about hackers and file damage. You're right to be concerned. Nothing is 100% safe on the internet. But besides the overwhelming advantage of having access to my files anywhere and everywhere, I have more faith that their backup systems are better maintained and more secure than my hard drive alone.

Although cloud storage has proven to be pretty darn secure, you can take a few extra steps to further protect yourself from a hacking or corruption event.

- Choose a well-known, proven provider with a worldwide reputation. If Dropbox goes down, it makes international news within minutes. If Joe's Cloud Storage Garage gets hacked, Joe just goes back to working at Starbucks… and you're out of luck.

- Enable two-factor authentication every single place it is offered.

  Did you get that? Every. Single. Place.

  Two-factor authentication is that system that sends you a code via email, phone or text when you log in to your systems (especially from an unknown browser or device). Taking this extra step is one of the smartest things you can do outside of upgrading your passwords (Page 126) to protect your accounts.

- Be smart about giving access to colleagues. It's fairly easy to set limitations on access to your files and folders. On Dropbox for example, you can set time limits on how long a link will be valid. Or you can let committee members read what's in a folder but not edit the files unless they download them and edit their own copy.

NerdHerd Thumbs Up:
Special Real Estate Tools

dotloop
Real Estate Document Manager
dotloop.com

My real estate followers always mention **dotloop** as an essential tool for creating, storing and managing the piles of documents their clients need to buy or sell properties. NerdHerder Steph Buell stores her contracts and documents in the system. "With dotloop, I can carry my office in my phone."

RPR
Real Estate Research Tool
narrpr.com

REALTORS® Property Resource, known as **RPR**, is a one-stop shop for real estate professionals, with aggregated facts and data about residential and commercial properties. NerdHerder Lynette Pendergast loves it because she says, "I can find properties near me or in any location in the country."

Organize and Store Photos and Video

· ·

The shoebox full of old photos has been replaced by a data-hogging digital folder of photos and video clips documenting soccer games, breakfasts and selfies. And both are still just as unorganized as ever. These tools help you organize, store and identify your photo memories.

Start with...

Google Photos   #CreepyButHelpful
Unlimited Photo/Video Storage with Image Recognition
google.com/photos

In 2016 **Google Photos** offered a great gift to the internet universe: free, unlimited photo storage for all. Besides the awesomeness of the free/unlimited feature, Google includes some positively eerie (creepy?) functionality that may forever change how you organize and find images.

Google groups photos by timelines and geography first, so you can look back to the pictures you took last April or just click on the New Orleans category to see your vacation photos from 2010.

Then it starts getting creepy. The service uses artificial intelligence through your photos and can identify faces and objects. My nephews kind of look alike. Not only did Google separate their pictures, it also identified the same boy from age 2 to age 9. Search for the word "dog," and images of your last three pets will appear on your page. It's not perfect by any stretch… many of my "dog" pictures were of my cats, Copy and Paste. I searched for "hat" and came up with all kinds of my family members and friends wearing hats. The word "orange" yielded a half dozen photos, and I know I have a bunch more.

When you click on the Assistant button, you'll discover a host of videos, collages and timelines that Google Photos created for you. You can also use their templates and search features to choose photos and videos to make creations of your own.

Then Try...

Amazon Prime Photos
Amazon's Answer to Google Photos
amazon.com/photos

If you have an Amazon Prime membership, the mega-seller offers **Prime Photos**, a Google Photo-like storage with image recognition functionality.

Shutterfly
Family-Friendly Online Photo Storage
shutterfly.com

My sister uses **Shutterfly** to share pics of my adorable nephews, and as well she should. This site is a safe place for schools and families to share kid photos, plus it has a robust series of tools to create photo books and gifts. Shutterfly products are more expensive than other options (see Photo Albums, Page 231), but my sister tells me the site is generous with coupons, and you can always check deal-finding sites (Page 168) for discount codes.

Also Check Out...

Photomyne
Photo-Scanning App for Photo Albums
photomyne.com

Wouldn't it be nice to dig through your old photo albums to find the great pics of you in middle school so you will win the #TBT hashtag on Throwback Thursdays?

Photomyne lets you snap a picture of multiple photos at once, like photos in a photo album. Then it automatically separates the photos into individual images for fine-tuning and sharing.

WedPics
Photo-Sharing App for Events
wedpics.com

From the title of this app, it's probably no secret that **WedPics** is geared toward weddings. The happy couple can set up a site and invite guests, who can then share the photos they take with the group. NerdHerder Johanne Stogran loves it. "WedPics offers an easy way to get informal, candid pictures of your wedding and all the festivities. Guests take them and then can share… it's a great way to share the day and it's FREE!"

Keep Track of Ideas

The amount of information that we need to stash away is increasing daily. We want to bookmark recipes, take notes at meetings, snag websites, store project photos and much more. These tools are arguably the best on the market for organizing bits and pieces of the world that we need to reference.

Start with...

Evernote
The Ultimate Note-Taking Tool
evernote.com

This is my fourth book on apps, and this is the fourth time I've declared that **Evernote** is the best note-taking tool. Though they've taken away some of the free features that we love, it's still the tool that stands out with the most features and integrations.

Evernote enables you to store pictures, documents, notes, webpages, snippets of text, handwritten doodles on napkins, emails and anything else you can possibly imagine. The search engine even combs through text in pictures (and in PDFs for Premium subscribers).

You can add your information to Evernote in every possible way as well—through browser plug-ins, email, web apps, desktop apps and mobile apps. When you have the information you want, you can tag it, organize it into folders, share it and search for it. The free version now limits you to two devices, but it's still the most feature rich.

Bring on the NerdHerd Evernote fans! Lucinda Harrison-Cox says, "It helps organize in one place so much of my work and personal digital life, including meeting notes, how to instructions, genealogy finds and to-do lists." Gianna Caruso agrees. "All notes for my life—both personal and professional—are all in one place. I can attach links from the web, add pictures and send them to anyone. It's a lifesaver." And a final note from Rita Tayenaka, "My favorite part is the business card integration with LinkedIn."

Then Try...

OneNote
Microsoft's Note-Taking Tool
onenote.com

Google Keep
Google's Note-Taking Tool
google.com/keep

Though Microsoft's **OneNote** preceded Evernote by 5 years, people didn't really start using it until the free version of Evernote took off and Microsoft made OneNote free. The two systems are fairly similar in that you can store anything and search for anything. OneNote obviously does a great job of integrating into the Microsoft suite of products, allowing users to throw bits of information into the system from any Microsoft program. **Google Keep** is also easy to use within Google's infrastructure, but both OneNote and Keep can stand on their own as well. Google Keep has fewer features than the other two top note-taking tools.

NerdHerder Kasey Nored likes the fact that you can add time and place reminders. "I can share my grocery list with my significant other so we can divide and conquer at the store with both of us getting live updates when items are checked off the list. The time or place reminders are spot on and so helpful because there are many days when I'm not sure what time I'll be where."

Also Check Out...

Apple Notes
Apple's Internal Note System
On Apple Devices

I have a rule that I don't write about one-platform tools, but I'm going to make an exception because **Apple Notes** is the note-taking tool that I use. It's nowhere near as robust as Evernote or OneNote, but it suits my needs perfectly. I take notes into the app on my phone, they're synchronized through iCloud to my Mac, and I can reach them on any browser. I can store photos, links, tasks, lists and regular old notes that are searchable from my device (not just inside the app).

Notability
NerdHerd Favorite Apple Notetaking App
gingerlabs.com

The only reason I didn't add **Notability** higher up in this list is because it's an Apple-only product, so I'm glad that NerdHerder Todd Fleischer listed it as his favorite tool.

Todd says,

> I love the integration of the app with my iPad Pro, where I can use my Apple Pencil to make notes on existing documents, file them away on a project/subject basis and import/export as needed. This one app has really allowed me to streamline what I take with me to meetings and saves time with everything in one place.

Simplenote
A Very Simple Note-Taking Tool
simplenote.com

If all you need to do with notes is to actually write notes (as opposed to saving multimedia, etc.), check out the lightweight tool **Simplenote**. It's very minimalistic, hence the "simple" name. But it's free, and people love it.

Take Meeting Notes

• •

Just because you have a great way to conduct a meeting doesn't mean your meeting is going to be productive. But you can make use of a couple of free tools to keep you and your meeting organized, on track and effective.

Start with...

Cisco Spark Meeting Notes

Meeting Organizer and Task Manager
notes.ciscospark.com

Cisco Spark Meeting Notes keeps an eye on your online calendar (Microsoft or Google) and sends you an email each day with a summary of the day's meetings as well as a reminder of yesterday's events and a reminder to add notes or tasks. The email contains a list of participants and a button to create an agenda, which lets you make your own or use one of their templates

When you take notes in Spark during the meeting, they're permanently captured and can be shared with other participants. You can also add new tasks and check on old tasks assigned to others.

Cisco Spark Meeting Notes can integrate into Trello (Page 38) and Slack (Page 55), and, believe it or not, Cisco Spark (Page 41) so your meetings coordinate with your project management tools.

Then Try...

AgreeDo

Meeting Management Tool with Agendas, Tasks, Minutes
  and Follow Up

agreedo.com

Before meetings, you can set an agenda in **AgreeDo** and invite attendees. During meetings, just keep the system open to take notes, record decisions, create action items and take attendance. After the meeting, everyone gets a copy of the notes as well as the tasks.

Also Check Out...

AudioNote

Voice Recorder with Synchronized Written Notes

luminantsoftware.com

Even if you take notes as fast as you can, it's easy to miss important points. **AudioNote** is a note-taking app that simultaneously records what's happening in the meeting. When you review your notes, you can play the audio from that moment in the meeting.

NerdHerder Kathy Wilson loves it.

> *When replaying the recording, I can select a particular note I've written, and AudioNote jumps to that place in the recording. It allows me to take the briefest notes so that I can truly pay attention and participate in discussions without missing anything. All of my meetings are stored in the cloud so I can access them anywhere. I'd be lost without it.*

Track Packages

● ●

It's your father's birthday, and he has yet to receive his "Birdwatchers Were the Original Tweeters" t-shirt you sent. But you don't have to rack your brain to try to remember the t-shirt shop's name to search for the receipt in your email. These apps keep track of your packages behind the scenes.

Start with...

Slice

Passive-Aggressive Package Tracker

slice.com

Slice is single-minded in focus. It sweeps through your cloud-based email (Gmail, AOL, Yahoo, etc.) to find all the receipts and shipping notifications. Then when you're trying to find a certain delivery, you can just open the app or go to the website to track every purchase and package.

A huge benefit of Slice is that it monitors the prices of your recent purchases and alerts you of price drops. I've saved hundreds of dollars from drops at Overstock.com and Nordstrom's with zero effort on my part. Slice will also let you know if a product you've purchased has been recalled.

Then Try...

Google Now   #CreepyButHelpful
Super Nosy Activity Monitor
google.com/now

EasilyDo
Package Tracker with Bonus Features
easilydo.com

Putting **Google Now** and **EasilyDo** into the Track Packages section is doing both a disservice, but tracking packages is certainly one of the strengths of these do-everything services. Google Now (or simply the Google app on Android devices) dives into your schedule, your travel plans, your purchases, your location and anything else it can see. EasilyDo is similar and adds email management as a bonus, plus helps you with contact management.

I think I'm supposed to like these two tools better than Slice, but I don't. EasilyDo seemed to disrupt my email more with its attempts at organization, and I didn't find it as helpful in tracking packages. Google Now is actually very helpful, and I use it for some of its other features, leaving the package tracking to Slice. You will appreciate how Google Now organizes your life into cards that you can flip through for snapshots of upcoming appointments, traffic alerts, packages, travel plans, weather and more.

Also Check Out...

Shyp
Shipping without the Hassle
shyp.com

We should all look forward to the day when **Shyp** is widely available rather than in just a few key cities. For a reasonable fee, Shyp will package anything you need to send, find the best rate for shipping and take the annoying task of physically putting your dad's gift in the mail off your plate.

Hot Topic:
Do Email Analysis Apps
Use Your Data?

Two of the tools that I love and recommend are Unroll.me (Page 134) and Slice (Page 27). And boy are people mad at them.

#CreepyButHelpful

An article in *The New York Times* about the ride-sharing app Uber outed Unroll.me for aggregating data from your purchases to sell to companies who want to know what you're doing. People were furious, prompting a mass deletion of both Unroll.me and Slice, its parent company.

But let's think about this for a minute. Unroll.me's actions do not come as a surprise to me. Although I can't say I was aware of the specific way they were benefitting from our relationship, I know that every time I let something have access to my email, photos, microphone, documents, etc., the company has access to my private life. The companies that offer cool, helpful tools such as Unroll.me are not run by trust-fund babies who are creating technology for the good of mankind. Most of them, like most of us, need to make money for the work we do in one way or another. Yes, there are a few developers who create a cool tool to share, but they are in the minority.

Remember this: if the product is free, you are the product.

Facebook collects mountains of data that it lets advertisers use to target you. Google used to read your emails and still tracks where you go on the web. The aggregation and sale of browsing history and interests are massive. If you're taking advantage of the good things the connected world has to offer, someone is taking advantage of you.

What can you do to protect your privacy?

I highly, highly, highly recommend you sign up for the free (and non-intrusive) email series called **The Privacy Paradox** (project.wnyc.org/privacy-paradox). The five emails give you simple steps to understand and examine your privacy options in today's tech world. When I listened to the series, I came to the conclusion that I'm comfortable with trading my data for the convenience that tech tools and services offer me. But you may not be. The first step is to listen to the series to become aware of what's happening. Then you can decide what, if anything, you want to do about it.

• •

NerdHerd Deluxe Edition!
Manager Molly Gardner's Top 10 Office Tools

Molly Gardner has managed Nerd HQ since 2014, and she's developed her own list of favorite tools that keep our company running. In her own words…

Working for Beth, a lot of apps and tools come across my desk. The ones you see here are my favorite tools that I use in the office day in and day out. This is the technology that keeps Nerd HQ running smoothly and Beth on the road bringing new ideas your way.

1. **Pomodoro One (Page 198)**

   My biggest priority (and struggle!) is staying focused. I use the **Pomodoro One** app to implement the Pomodoro Technique—working for intervals of 25 minutes with a 5-minute break. This simple tomato icon in the corner of my browser keeps me on task.

2. **Todoist (Page 7)**

   Hands down, **Todoist** is the tool I can't live without. More than a to-do list, I manage my day, my projects and our clients using this life-changing system. It's simple, it's affordable and it works.

3. Google Calendar (Page 2)

Using an online calendar system I trust gives me peace of mind and I've never had an issue with **Google Calendar**. It integrates seamlessly with several of my other favorites (TripIt, Todoist, and our customer relationship manager tool [CRM]).

4. TripIt (Page 138)

Beth sometimes travels to 3 or 4 cities in a week. Using **TripIt**, I'm confident she won't lose a hotel confirmation and she can stay on top of her flight changes. We utilize the notes field to give her a handy place to see information on the upcoming event, even when she's offline.

5. Wave

Online Small Business Accounting
waveapps.com

We use **Wave** for our office's bookkeeping. I can create an invoice in less than a minute, and our clients like the ability to pay via credit card and download an instant receipt. The system is free and intuitive. We can't figure out why no one knows about it.

6. Square

Payment Processing Via Smartphones or Online
squareup.com

Wave does the trick for most large payments, but **Square** is a great way to create an easy-to-use online store for Beth's books, collectors cards and Beth-in-a-Box.

7. Fancy Hands (Page 160)

Cross your little tasks off the list by passing them onto the assistants at **Fancy Hands**. Someone is always ready to research the best product, make a doctor's appointment or even upload business cards to your database.

ORGANIZE

8. Canva (Page 248)

I am not a designer, but I can whip up a professional-looking social media image or an email header in minutes using **Canva**. The templates make anyone look like a pro and you can easily share your designs with your team for feedback and edits.

9. Dropbox (Page 14)

I keep everything in **Dropbox**. It is a safe way to store, organize and share your files online.

10. Genius Scan (Page 111)

Skip wrestling with your printer and scan a document from your mobile device using **Genius Scan**.

Bonus Tool!
Proposify
Upscale Proposal Creation and Tracking
proposify.biz

With **Proposify**, you can present your clients with a beautiful, branded online proposal. As an added plus, you'll be notified when they view the document and when you win their business. It's pricier than most of the tools that Beth shares, but we put this into the category of #WorthThePrice.

Collaborate

I want to . . .

Collaborate on Files

• •

Remember the days when you sent everyone a copy of a document for feedback, then you had to read each version and compile the feedback into one file? Yeah, I've blocked out those dark times, too. These tools offer real-time collaboration and sharing for teams and committees.

Start with...

Google Drive

Real-Time Collaboration in a Robust Office Suite
google.com/drive

Oh, the glory that is **Google Drive**. It's hands down the best and easiest free tool for document collaboration out there. You can create or upload word docs, spreadsheets and slides, then invite collaborators to edit and comment. The best feature is that you can see the updates made by any contributor in real time. Collaborators can participate even if they're not Google users, though if they are, the system will identify them by name.

Although Google Drive doesn't have the most features or the best interface, the free collaboration features earn my thumbs up for this category. (But not for overall office suites... my heart is still with Microsoft Office.

Then Try...

Microsoft Office 365

Office Suite with Collaboration Features
microsoft.com/office365

I so want **Microsoft Office 365** to be as easy as Google Drive for collaboration, but it's just not. When you're working in your Microsoft document on your computer, you can share it with collaborators with a click. But those guys will be working with your document through

COLLABORATE

the online version of the software, and you're not going to be able to see their changes until you refresh your page. If you're editing in a browser, the site will automatically save every few seconds, so other comments will show up after a delay.

Also Check Out...

Folia
Clean File-Sharing Site for Feedback from Teams
folia.com

From the makers of iAnnotate we have **Folia**, a web-based tool for sharing files for feedback and markup. If you need to share a document with others but don't want them to be able to download a copy or really change anything, this quick tool lets people you invite markup a document and add comments. The annotations are updated in real time so everyone in the document sees the new notes. Collaborators have to register, which is a bummer, but it's a nice alternative for your Google-hatin' committee members who don't want to use Google Drive.

NerdHerd Thumbs Up: GoToMyPC

GoToMyPC
Remote Access Tool
gotomypc.com

When you can't store everything in the cloud so you can work on any device, you may need to access your main computer from afar. **GoToMyPC** is NerdHerder Emily Garner's favorite tool for this. "I can work from my desktop from anywhere—including my phone."

Share Large Files

• •

Dropbox and other cloud-based storage systems (Page 14) make it pretty easy to share links to large files, but you may need other choices from time to time.

Start with...

WeTransfer
Easy File-Sharing Service
wetransfer.com

There's nothing fancy about **WeTransfer's** services, and there doesn't have to be. You choose a file to upload (up to 2GB free), and drag it to the screen. Then it uploads. And you share it. And you're done without having to throw a USB drive into the mail.

Then Try...

DropSend
Classic File-Sharing Tool
dropsend.com

MediaFire
File-Sharing Service for Media Files
mediafire.com

In my extremely unscientific trials of the tools in this section, WeTransfer uploaded files faster than many other tools, but the others have their benefits. **DropSend** has been around for a while. It's solid, proven and darn easy.

MediaFire's free version gives you plenty of free storage, and the one-time-use links are perfect when you don't want to grant unlimited use of your content.

Also Check Out...

Balloon
File Sharing for Dropbox
balloon.io

Balloon is a whimsical site that works with Dropbox (Page 14). You create folder names that they call "balloons," and send the link to anyone who needs to send you something. Then the sharer just drags files into the balloon, and you get them in your Dropbox. For added security, you can add a password to your balloon.

Hot Topic:
Shorten Long URLs with Bitly

Bitly
URL Shortener
bitly.com

If the link you're sharing is long and cumbersome, a quick visit to **Bitly** will morph the complicated URL into something short and easy to type. NerdHerder Dottie France from the Piedmont Regional Association of REALTORS® gives it a thumbs up, as do I. We at Nerd HQ use Bitly with custom tokens to transform a rat's nest of a URL.

https://www.amazon.com/
Beth-Ziesenis/e
/B004YWLF4A/
ref=sr_ntt_srch_lnk_1?
qid=1495901640&sr=8-1

nerdybff.com/BethZonAmazon

Manage Projects

The project management world is a crowded space, but a few companies stand out. These tools are the most recommended by audience members in my sessions, and those guys are way smarter than I am.

Like the cloud storage tools, you'll find many of the same characteristics in the top contenders. In general, here are the features these tools contain:

- Capability to set up projects with tasks, goals and milestones
- Collaboration tools for teams
- Feeds and dashboards for latest activity and status updates
- Ability to assign tasks to team members
- Shareable file library
- Notification system via email or third-party tools
- Multi-device access to cloud-based data
- Free or low-cost basic features with upgrades for larger teams and projects

Beyond these common characteristics, you'll find variety in the look and feel of the most popular tools.

Start with...

Trello
Project Management Tool Good for Personal Task Management
trello.com

Trello offers an interesting take on project management by organizing your projects into "cards" that lay out like a deck across your screen. You can click on any card to flip it over and see the details, including tasks, collaborators and due dates.

Trello organizes all your projects into boards, allowing both personal and shared boards. Your account lets you have as many boards as you want, and you can manage the permissions for each for everything from read-only access to full privileges. You create lists and deadlines for each board, and you can assign tasks to others. It's easy to reprioritize and assign list items with a quick click and drag.

Trello gets bonus points because it has personality: a sense of playfulness as well as serious business features. You can choose bright, fun backgrounds for your projects, and a "Power-Up" feature (that doesn't even cost more money) lets your older cards show their age. Plus, the Pirate View is what you need in your life.

COLLABORATE

Then Try...

Asana
Favorite Project Management Tool with Robust Free Version
asana.com

Smartsheet
Spreadsheet-Based Project Management Tool
smartsheet.com

Asana and **Smartsheet** are crowd favorites at my sessions. Many teams report that Asana gives small teams everything they need at no cost for up to 15 users. And although Smartsheet isn't free, its users adore the fact that the system has templates for almost any type of project, and the layout is the familiar spreadsheet format.

NerdHerder Pamela Lewis says, "Smartsheet keeps me on top of all the 'busy' things that need to be taken care of so they don't fall thought the cracks in the parking lot!"

Also Check Out...

Basecamp
Classic Project Management System
basecamp.com

In 2004, a company called 37signals started creating online project management systems, primarily for the web design industry. **Basecamp** has evolved to be one of the most popular web-based project collaboration tools to share files, meet deadlines, assign tasks, centralize feedback and finish what you start.

Basecamp is probably the management services with the most integrations, including social networks, mobile phones and invoicing software. All the systems update each other and keep everyone on track. The company has changed its pricing structure multiple times since I started using it, but it looks like they've settled on $99 a month flat rate. One seriously cool benefit of Basecamp is that it's completely free for teachers and half price for nonprofits.

Freedcamp
(Almost) Free Project Management System
freedcamp.com

Unlimited users. Unlimited projects. Unlimited storage. What's not to love? **Freedcamp** gives away much more than many of the other top project management systems in this section. They start charging for integrations with Google Drive, larger file uploads, CRMs, invoices and issue tracking.

Podio
Customizable Project Management System
podio.com

Podio has the most flexibility when it comes to personalizing a tool to organize your business, but I find it the most complicated. You can add all kinds of things, such as events, inventory and projects. The set-up process is a little confusing, and every time I've gone to create a project, I give up and just use something else. If you have the patience, it's a very powerful business and project management tool.

Meet Virtually

Phone calls are so 2007. These days we feel more connected with teams when we hear, see and participate in our remote meetings. Here are five scenarios for meeting with people from afar that brings them closer together.

Cisco Spark
Online Meeting Tools with Meeting Management
ciscospark.com

FaceTime
Apple's Videoconferencing Tool
apple.com/facetime

FreeConferenceCall.com
Free Conference Calling
freeconferencecall.com

Google Hangouts
Google's Online Meeting Tool
google.com/hangouts

GoToMeeting/GoToWebinar
Pioneer Online Meeting Tool
gotomeeting.com

Join.Me
Instant Screensharing Tool
join.me

Skype
Perhaps the Original Online Meeting/Chat Tool—Now with Instant Translation
skype.com

COLLABORATE

UberConference
Conference Call Tool with Hi-Tech Features
uberconference.com

WebEx
Another Classic Online Meeting Tool
webex.com

Zoom
HD Videoconferencing Tool
zoom.us

1. **"Let me show you what I'm talking about."**

   I've long admired the beautiful simplicity of **Join.me**. It's perfect for a quick one-to-one collaboration to literally get someone else on the same page. Sometimes people write me with a tech question, and instead of trying to write an answer, I simply say, "Jump on a Join.me and I'll show you." Join.me lets you join from a computer or several mobile apps. It's a tiny little download that takes a sec or two to install. The basic version is free and lets you show your screen to up to 10 people, and 5 of those can be brought in via video.

2. **"Let's plow into this project together."**

   Despite some advances that Microsoft is making in the world of real-time document collaboration, **Google Drive** (Page 34) still wins in this category. It's incredibly easy to jump on a call and talk to team members while you all add ideas to a Google Doc. Sometimes when I'm working with a client on a new presentation idea, we both throw verbiage down on the same page and hash things out in minutes rather than emailing drafts back and forth for days.

3. "We need a face-to-face meeting."

You have lots of choices for video conferencing these days: good ole' **Skype**, sometimes reliable (but improving) **Google Hangouts** and even **FaceTime**. But my new favorite professional tool is **Zoom**, which lets you pull in up to 50 HD video streams at the same time. Meetings have a time limit for the free version, but you can look at this as a benefit. Imagine saying, "We're trying to save the organization money, so we're using the free version, which means that this meeting must last less than 40 minutes!" Everyone will love you.

4. "Our meetings are inefficient. Let's use a better collaboration tool."

Cisco Spark's instant meeting capabilities include video and audio options, but the integration with Cisco Spark Meeting Notes (Page 25) makes the tool well suited for collaboration via meetings.

5. "The last time we had a video conference, Jim forgot to wear pants. We're going back to teleconferences."

I still find myself on a number of teleconferences when I get together with a committee to talk about an upcoming event. **Freeconferencecall** is just that... free conference calls. I've heard from a few people that the connections can be a little unreliable, but I've always had good luck. Bonus: Freeconferencecall now has free online meetings for up to 25 people. I haven't tried the online meetings out yet, but cool!

For a different take on teleconferences, try **UberConference**. They have a free version, but the coolest feature is in the paid level ($120 a year): The system calls out to participants at the designated time, so no more pin numbers. Another bonus: If you have traditional conference calls with PINs and annoyances, try MeetingMogul (Page 69).

6. **"We need to share this with our members. Let's do a webinar."**

You have plenty of options in this area, and many of them are pretty pricy. The good news is that **GoToMeeting/GoToWebinar** and **WebEx** have both recognized the crazy competition in their markets, and their prices are quite reasonable these days. I find both platforms reliable and flexible—the only challenge I have is that they both update their software frequently, and almost every time I do a webinar I have to install a new version. Meh.

Also Check Out...

Appear.in
Instant Video Conferencing with Screensharing
appear.in

Hmmm. In researching this book, I think I found a tool I like better than my beloved Join.me. **Appear.in** is absolutely adorable. On the home page, just click to start a meeting with a randomly generated link, and seconds later you're staring at your own reflection in a chat room. Share the link with up to 8 others for instant collaboration and screensharing. Participants on mobile devices must download a free app.

The adorable part comes in with the emoji buttons. You can post a thumbs up or a smiley face bashing its head against a brick wall… whatever suits your mood.

Communicate

· ·

I want to . . .

Jazz Up Presentations

For—I don't know, 200 years?—the standard for presentations has been Microsoft's PowerPoint. Ever since we dropped the overhead projector/ transparency model, we've emphasized key points of our educational sessions with hard-to-read, badly designed bullet-point slides.

Although PowerPoint is still the most popular program, it has become the software we love to hate. That's why we're always looking for alternatives.

Start with...

Prezi

Storytelling PowerPoint Alternative

prezi.com

The concept of **Prezi** is innovative. Pretend you have a giant white-board with all your information for your presentation. As the presenter, you have a high-quality video camera. As you tell your story, you zoom in and out of relevant areas of the whiteboard, even rotating the camera into new areas to draw people's attention to the right elements, then pulling back to show the big picture.

As with PowerPoint, your content will be organized by slides, even though the final Prezi looks nothing like a slide-based presentation. Each slide represents where your Prezi will move next.

The free version of Prezi lets you create public presentations and share them online. For $59 a year, you can keep your Prezis private, and $159 gets you the software to create Prezis without an internet connection.

Sway

Microsoft PowerPoint Alternative… Created by Microsoft

sway.com

Believe it or not, one of the coolest new PowerPoint alternatives comes from… the creator of PowerPoint. **Sway** is a sleek presentation tool that enables you to create a slide deck that's more like a flowing website, including dynamic content like embedded videos and social media posts. You can use it in place of traditional slides or let it stand alone.

Then Try...

Google Slides

Google's PowerPoint Alternative
slides.google.com

Although I'm still not in love with the **Google Slides** templates, the online tool is easy to use and can be convenient for presenting on the go. Tip: Check out Envato (Page 247) for presentation templates that don't suck.

Emaze

Creative Online Presentations Plus Website Building
emaze.com

You will love the innovative templates with **Emaze**, a Prezi/ PowerPoint-type mashup. You create the presentations on the website, but a paid subscription will enable you to download your presentation to give your talk offline. Emaze recently added a feature that lets you create innovative personal websites, but at the time of this printing, the sites looked horrible on mobile devices. I bet they fix that soon.

Haiku Deck

Presentation Tools Heavy on the Graphics
haikudeck.com

Haiku Deck provides beautiful, easy-to-use templates for presentations on the iPad and the web. The clean look of the templates is perfect for the minimalist design trends we see in today's best presentations.

Office Mix
PowerPoint Plugin to Create Interactive Presentations
mix.office.com

With this free plugin for PowerPoint, you can create interactive presentations with voiceover narration and even your bright, smiling face playing on the screen. **Office Mix** lets you add polling, sections, annotations and more interactive features to PowerPoint slides. The videos can then be hosted on the web and embedded into sites. The interactive features work well for viewers online and on mobile devices. These videos are perfect for training or lessons. I kinda can't believe it's free.

Visme
Creative Presentations and Infographics
visme.co

I have mixed feelings about including **Visme** in this list. On one hand, Visme looks creative, innovative and different, with cool tools like social media integration and great animations. The site also includes templates for infographics and social media graphics, which makes Visme good for one-stop creativity.

On the other hand . . . gosh—they make it so hard to try out. Almost everything that looks interesting is behind the paywall (starting at $10 a month). The basic templates are soooo very basic that I didn't have the opportunity to see how cool it might be. And I wasn't willing to pay ten bucks to find out.

Also Check Out...

Issuu
Online Magazine Maker
issuu.com

Have you ever created a fantastic PowerPoint and saved it into that boring 4-slide-per-page handout? The mystical, magical site called

Issuu transforms your boring handout into an interactive, dynamic, interesting online magazine, book or catalog that people can flip through. The graphics of the viewing interface will make you look like a pro, and it has built-in features that allow readers to share and download your files.

Transforming your boring document into an online magazine is embarrassingly simple. Just drag a file to the uploader, name your document, add a description and press a button. Issuu will process your file in no time and then provide you with everything you need to share your new magazine.

NerdHerder Michele Huber says Issuu makes her publications look awesome. "I love it because it's easy to share with my members. It is interactive and very professional looking, and as a one-person office, that's important to me."

Hot Topic:
Stop Killing People with
Boring PowerPoint

PowerPoint doesn't have to be ugly. My secret weapon for making beautiful slide decks is the Envato Marketplace, a gallery of easy-to-personalize templates for presentations, blogs and much, much more. See more about Envato on Page 247.

Schedule Meetings with Individuals

• •

Going back and forth with a contact to find a time to meet is a waste of her time and yours. Book your appointments without the hassle using a little tech touch.

Start with...

X.ai   #CreepyButHelpful

Virtual Scheduling Assistant (Who Doesn't Exist)

x.ai

Artificial intelligence technology is EXPLODING! I read articles every day about how computers can "think" more and more. They can recognize faces in your photos (Google Photos, Page 19), interpret your conversations (Translation Tools, Pages 84 and 85), learn from your habits, predict your needs (Google Now, Page 28) and much more. It's creepy, yes. But it's helpful. And, like it or not, it's coming. Fast.

X.ai offers a virtual scheduling assistant, a "person" named Amy Ingram (for AI, get it?). Amy has a brother named Andrew, if you'd rather have a male assistant. To schedule a meeting with a contact or small group, copy Amy on your emails. Amy will email your contacts directly to find a time to meet. She "reads" meeting requests and responses as you write them in natural language. After people settle on a good time, she sends an invite to everyone. I put Amy to the test during a free trial period, and she worked so well (for the most part) that many of my invitees forgot that she wasn't real even though I told them.

You'll find x.ai competitors popping up more and more, but this tool seems to be the most reasonably priced with a starting monthly price of $39 or up to five meetings per month for free.

Then Try...

YouCanBook.Me
Do-It-Themselves Scheduling Tool
youcanbook.me

Sometimes it's just easier to send your calendar to someone and have her pick her preferred appointment time. **YouCanBook.Me** has a free plan that's so easy, it makes sense to sign up even if you don't need to use it often.

The system connects to your online calendar (like Google or iCloud) and shows open slots available for meetings. Your meeting partner can choose the slot she wants, then she adds her name and email for automatic reminders and a downloadable confirmation. She can use the confirmation link to update or cancel the appointment as well.

Calendly
The Scheduling App My Colleagues Adore
calendly.com

When my fellow speakers start chatting about scheduling and calendar tools, the fans of **Calendly** go wild with exclamation points. The pricing, features and functionality look about the same as YouCanBook.Me, with the added benefit of a plethora of integrations with other apps such as Zapier (Page 157) and GoToMeeting (Page 41).

Timebridge
In Case You Don't Like Calendly or YouCanBook.Me
timebridge.com

Timebridge is yet another scheduler that does the same kind of stuff. But this one is 100% free, even with multiple calendar integrations and your own branding.

Assistant.to

NerdHerd Favorite Scheduler

assistant.to

New NerdHerd member Lisa Braithwaite likes the convenience of the Gmail integration of **Assistant.to** for her speaker clients. "With Assistant.to, the client selects a time from within the email, and we both get notifications. I don't even have to send them to another site. Super easy."

Hot Topic:
You Can Automate Your
Scheduling... But Should You?

Once upon a time I had an immediate need for a freelancer. A colleague gave me a recommendation. I tried to call the freelancer for a quick chat and left a message, followed by a detailed email. She wrote me back and asked me to fill out an intake sheet, which asked for the same details I had already emailed. I pasted the answers into her form then asked again for a quick call. Instead she sent yet another link to a scheduling calendar, and the first timeslot that would work with my schedule was 3 weeks out.

So, I called another freelancer. And she answered the phone. And I hired her.

Although automated scheduling tools can be handy, putting up with a little inconvenience by personally booking your appointments may pay off in the end.

Thus ends my little moral tale.

Schedule Meetings with Groups

How may emails does it take to set up a committee meeting? One, if you use one of these cool tools that help you find a time to meet.

Start with...

WhenIsGood

Easy Way to Find a Time to Meet
whenisgood.net

WhenIsGood will make you look organized to your colleagues, even though the interface looks like it was created in 2002. Create an event and choose potential meeting times by dragging your mouse over blocks of time. Then send the link to your participants, and they can paint in their availability so the system can identify a common time when all participants can meet. It's easy and fast. I just wish it was more modern looking.

Then Try...

Doodle

Everybody's Favorite Scheduling Tool
doodle.com

Every time I ask for favorite apps in my presentations, **Doodle** comes up. Besides having an adorable name, it's dead simple to use. Without ever entering your email address or any personal information (making it commitment free), you can propose several dates and times for a meeting. Then Doodle generates a link for both your admin view and the participants' responses. You send the link to your participants, and everyone responds with availability, allowing you to use the admin view to find the perfect time. "It's a time saver," adds NerdHerder Anne Blackman.

I have used it for years, but recently Doodle upped its game to make it even more valuable. Now you can use the apps to check on your schedules and propose more meetings. Plus, it's added a MeetMe page that gives you a private URL you can send to colleagues to let them propose a time to meet based on your availability.

Also Check Out...

SignUpGenius
Volunteer Organizer
signupgenius.com

SignUpGenius is NerdHerder Celia Fritz-Watson's favorite tech tool. The tool's main purpose is to help groups organize who is doing what and when, letting volunteers sign up for tasks and time slots. And Celia says it helps her find times for groups to meet. "SignUpGenius allows a group of people to set up a meeting time and date easily, without the hassle of tons of reply all emails going back and forth."

NerdHerd Thumbs Up: Parliamentary Tools

Magic Gavel
App to Manage Official Meeting
    Using Official Rules
greatmeeting.com/magic-gavel

NerdHerder Colette Collier Trohan actually created this app, but it's definitely worth mentioning. **Magic Gavel** helps you conduct official proceedings like board meetings. It calculates votes, helps you run the meeting and gives you a quick reference to parliamentary procedures. "We wrote it to help people stay on track during meetings. They can get quick answers about procedures and back to the subject at hand."

Communicate with Internal Teams

At times in the world of technology, we see giant leaps and dramatically new ways of doing things. Smartphones forever changed the center of our computing universe from a desktop machine to devices that are with us all the time. Cloud storage tools (Page 13) transformed the way we store and share files. Social media platforms altered the very way we live our lives and interact with others. And tools like these internal communication systems have the potential of weaning us off email in the office.

Start with...

Slack
Simple Chat System with Monumental Capabilities
slack.com

Slackreview.com
Directory of Slack Apps and Integrations
slackreview.com

In the simplest terms, **Slack** is instant messaging. The system connects teams and allows them to send quick messages on almost any platform, avoiding the annoying email strings that we've all learned to ignore. The chats can be tagged for different topics and created for different groups inside the same network. It's basically a social network for the workplace, as well as the perfect setup for sports teams, volunteer committees, church groups and community discussions.

But Slack is really so much more. Just visit **Slackreview.com** to see hundreds of apps and integrations that exponentially expand Slack's capabilities. Teams can use Slack for…

- Project management (who is supposed to do what and when?)
- Employee recognition (award your favorite team members virtual tacos when they do something awesome)
- Lunch coordination (who wants what from the Thai place?)
- IT system monitoring (IT guys love to monitor stuff)
- Videoconferencing (don't just type to your team… see them)
- Weather (let Poncho the Cat tell you when to bring an umbrella)
- Transportation (order a Lyft)

There's even an integration to create a group Swear Jar.

Tech companies were the first organizations to embrace Slack, but look for it to extend to other industries soon, especially since Microsoft and other providers are developing their own Slack-like communication tools. Slack has a free version to let you try it out. A couple of challenges to a successful Slack rollout for your team: You'll have to get buy-in from your whole team, and convincing some people to step away from email can be tough. You may also be annoyed by all the notifications. But the benefits may outweigh the drawbacks when you see your email inbox shrink to a manageable size and notice that your teams are finally working together better to get stuff done.

Two NerdHerders listed Slack as their favorite tool. Pam Donahoo says Slack makes it easy to set up channels and allows file sharing and communication among teams. Pam is the executive director of American Mensa, so she probably knows smart stuff when she sees it. And Doris Nurenberg adds, "My staff and I work virtually 95% of the time, and the app allows us to share ideas, collaborate and most importantly, log calls with customers. We all know what the calls are about, how they were answered who we talked to and how to pick up the conversation if we take the next call from the same caller."

Then Try...

HipChat.com
Slack Alternative
hipchat.com

Samepage
Well-Regarded Slack Alternative
samepage.io

Fleep.io
Slack Alternative with Easier User Additions
fleep.com

Because Slack is so dang popular, the competition is fierce. **HipChat** and **Samepage** offer variations on the theme with a few different features. **Fleep** stands out because you don't have to ask others to sign in to the system… just communicate with outsiders using their email address. Plus it has the best name.

Also Check Out...

Facebook Workplace
Facebook's Answer to Slack
workplace.fb.com

Facebook Workplace is counting on the fact that millions of us sneak peeks at Facebook during the workday. The drawback is that the system works separately from your personal Facebook page, so you'll have to have two accounts.

Microsoft Teams

Slack Competitor for Microsoft Business Users

teams.microsoft.com

Microsoft is being a little stingy with its Slack competitor because it's only for companies that use Office 365 business plans, and right now you can't invite people without Office 365 subscriptions to join in on the party. Nevertheless, the development of **Microsoft Teams** shows just how popular Slack has become.

Microsoft Teams is very much like Slack, with the ability to create channels, add fun, instantly communicate and easily collaborate. And because it's fully integrated into the Office 365 infrastructure, users can share, chat, collaborate and create inside any Office product without messing around with a third-party tool.

Hot Topic:
Where Did All the .Coms Go?

In the old days, like 2014, most sites ended with a traditional .com, .org or, if they were hip, .net. So where the heck did .io come from, and what does it signify?

The Internet Corporation for Assigned Names and Numbers (ICANN) creates and manages domain extensions, known as top-level domains (TLDs). They've created hundreds and hundreds of options, with more releases every year.

TLDs can fall into several categories, including generic domains (.com), restricted domains (.gov), sponsored domains (.museum) and country domains (.uk). Here are a few domains that may help you recognize sites that deal with technology:

- .ai
  The country of Anguilla owns .ai, which has been adopted for sites that deal with artificial intelligence.

- .io
  This TLD is actually the country code for the British Indian Ocean Territory, but startups love it.

- .bz
  I thought I was so clever to lock up the domain   #NerdFail
  nerdy.bz, which I wanted people to read as
  "nerdy dot Beth Z." But even my manager thought
  the .bz stood for business. The domain belongs to Belize.

- .co
  Colombia owns .co, but you'll see many tech companies using it.

- Emoji Domains
  Believe it or not, you can register a domain that uses emojis. The domain uses the TLD .ws, which comes from Samoa. Hurry! The nerd-lovers' site 💜 🕶 💜 .ws is still available as of this printing.

Broadcast Live Video

Real-time video broadcasts have been around for quite some time, but until very recently, they were pretty much unknown. Meerkat introduced its Twitter-feed broadcasts at SXSW in 2015, and Twitter promptly destroyed it by releasing Periscope right after. Since then we've seen a growth in the market for live broadcasting and the ways you can do it.

Here are three ways, old and new, to share real-time video with the world.

Start with...

Periscope

Twitter's Live Video Tool

periscope.tv

To broadcast live on Twitter, you need a Twitter account, and you just push a button and start speaking to the world. People can view your feed and send comments as well as little hearts to show affection.

I jumped into **Periscope** right away when it first released, and I decided I'm not a huge fan (although NerdHerder Denise M. Smith loves it). First, I don't necessarily like the one-way communication. I find myself staring at the camera on my phone and blabbering on. When people ask questions or come on, I give shoutouts. But for the most part, I bet I'm pretty boring to watch.

And speaking of boring, I quit watching   #NerdFail
Periscope the day that a woman was 'scoping
while grocery shopping with her kids, and about 60 of us were with her as she picked out cereal. Really? People were giving advice on brands and she was just talking out loud to herself (to us, really) about her groceries. Another mind-numbing stream showed a famous tech blogger working on a story: About 140 people were watching this man silently type and stare at his screen. Come on.

Another challenge that I've had with Periscope in particular is with trolls. Although you can limit your live feeds to your followers if your account is private, you'll probably have a very limited audience (maybe just your mom?). If you broadcast to the world, you're going to come across trolls.

Trolls are horrible people who hang out on social media sites and make it a point to get under other people's skins. Once I was broadcasting an awards ceremony where a college student was receiving accolades. A troll on the Twitter feed started saying cruel things about this beautiful student's appearance, and I quickly shut the stream down. Who the hell would do that?

On the positive side, I've seen people's streams from breaking news sites, like when a building was on fire in NYC. I've also seen people stream speeches from events or give meaningful feedback on current events. And then there are the guys who stream on their commutes to work and say absolutely nothing of substance. Meh.

Then Try...

Facebook Live
Facebook's Live Video Tool
live.fb.com

Even though **Facebook Live** is like Periscope in that it's basically a one-way communication, I see more potential there. First, you can limit the broadcasts to your own peeps, which means that you probably won't have random trolls saying horrible things. Second, I love that Facebook loves its own video so much that it bumps a live post up in everyone's feeds so your post gets priority, even when the stream is over. On your professional pages, this increased exposure will be helpful for reaching your audiences.

Google Hangouts On Air/YouTube Live Stream

Google's Live Video Tool

plus.google.com/hangouts/onair

Google Hangouts has a cool setting that lets you broadcast a video conference live to **YouTube**, and YouTube itself has a live broadcast feature. This means that you can share your panel discussion of industry trends with your membership base, or even broadcast your family reunion to the people who couldn't make the trip.

Also Check Out...

Tunity

App that Routes Live TV Audio Through Your Device

tunity.com

Tunity is a free app that lets you stream the audio from live TV channels through your mobile device. This gives you the freedom to watch a muted TV and hear the audio on your own.

Connecting Tunity takes seconds... just put the TV in the scan area on your phone, and if the channel is supported, you'll be listening in less than 30 seconds. You'll have to enable location services so the app will find the right feed. It works with about 100 basic cable channels on live TV only, so sorry, no Netflix.

I've found myself using it all over the place, from the waiting area at an airport gate to a hotel room when I didn't want to bother other guests with my blaring TV. And when I told my husband about this tool, he immediately asked me to download it to his phone. In marriage terms, that's a win!

NerdHerd Thumbs Up:
Snapchat

Snapchat
Social Media Tool for the Cool Kids
snapchat.com

NerdHerder Gina Jones says her favorite app is **Snapchat**, so I'll include it for her sake. But I just want to say publicly that I really don't get it. I have two teenage girls as Snapchat connections, but they don't send me anything. And when they do, it just disappears. So I just don't get it. Yes, I know that Snapchat Stories are a way to share moments of your life. And it's cool to use the augmented reality filters that give you bunny ears and bug eyes. And I know brands create great Snapchat geofilters and channels to help their social media presence. But I look at my empty Snapchat inbox and feel sad and lonely. Like middle school. #NerdyPityParty

Manage Email

The best thing to happen to us as professionals is that we can get email wherever we go.

The worst thing to happen to us as professionals is that we can get email wherever we go.

Here are some of my favorite tools to make our email inboxes a little less horrible.

Start with...

Gmail
Versatile Email Platform
google.com/gmail

Inbox by Gmail
Google's Extra Special Email Management App
google.com/inbox

Gmailify
Feature to Use Gmail Tools with Non-Gmail Accounts
In Gmail App

In my humble opinion, **Gmail** is the strongest tool in my fight against email madness. Not only can you import all your email accounts into the Gmail system (and send them from the different accounts as well), Gmail filters spam better than any tool I've used. In addition, Gmail's integration with about a kabillion tools means that I can extend the functionality to manage my travel, organize my to-dos, track my packages, research my contacts and much, much, much more.

NerdHerder Andrew Hartman agrees with me about Gmail's helpfulness. "I can control personal and business email from one app."

Gmail has a standard inbox, but **Inbox by Gmail** has the email triage tools you'll find in the Microsoft Outlook app, such as automatic sorting and instant responses.

And if you don't want to get into the Google infrastructure, Gmail now offers the best of its features for Yahoo, AOL, Outlook, Hotmail and other non-Gmail accounts. Just install the **Gmailify** app and link your email accounts.

COMMUNICATE

Then Try...

Microsoft Outlook
Email Triage Tool
microsoft.com/outlook

Once upon a time I was a Microsoft girl, and if there was any tool that would get me to return to Windows, it's **Microsoft Outlook**. Not only do I love the rules that helped me organize my inbox (Gmail's aren't as good), but I also adore the Microsoft Outlook app.

Like Gmail, you can consolidate all your other email accounts into the Outlook app. Then the fun begins. Use the app to schedule emails, find times to meet, attach files and swipe and scan your way through your inbox on the go. Best of all, the mobile app and all its advanced features is free, which means you can use it on the go while still keeping your main email system, such as Gmail or Yahoo.

Also Check Out...

SaneBox
Email Management Tool with Bonus Features
sanebox.com

SaneBox goes beyond just email management. You can use it to unsubscribe from both mailing lists and individual senders (maybe your crazy aunt who sends you emails about angels?), which goes beyond Unroll.me's tools (Page 134). You can also filter your sent mail to see people who haven't written back. It's not a separate app, you just add it to your present email system and let it learn what emails are important to you and what you can trash.

The tool also lets you remind yourself to follow up and can schedule emails to come back to you at a later time (Outlook and Gmail do some of that, too). SaneBox starts at $7 a month. I like the way they explain the price: "There's an old saying 'If you're not paying for a product, then you are the product.' You are our customer—not our product."

Jazz Up Email

• •

How many emails do you get a day? Bet they all look the same. To stand out in someone's inbox, you need to do something a little different.

Start with...

BombBomb

Video Email System

bombbomb.com

Oh gosh. This email tool could be a game changer. **BombBomb** is a video email tool that lets you send video emails that are embedded into the message. The attractive format creates a clean, inviting email for your contacts. Each video has a big play button and the video length listed.

The Google Chrome plugin takes over your Gmail (Page 64) page but adds lots of helpful sales tools, such as email tracking. And you can click one button to dash off a quick, personal video. You can also create a bank of videos for automated replies (such as follow-up requests, etc.).

BombBomb starts at about $40 a month, a little on the pricey side compared to most tools in this book. But I'm going to put it into the category of worth the price for sales and customer service folks.

Then Try...

CloudHQ Video Email

Video Email for Gmail

nerdybff.com/cloudhqvideoemail

If the price of BombBomb scares you off, give this free Chrome plugin a try. CloudHQ is some sort of backup service, but they've also put out a ton of free plugins. It took me a few minutes to figure out how to sign up for **CloudHQ Video Email** while avoiding their other (paid) services. But after I installed it, I was able to send a video email in seconds.

The system lets you record a video from your Gmail (Page 64) compose screen. One easy option is to upload the video to your YouTube account and embed it in the email. The YouTube video is private, so only people with the links can view. One weird thing… when your contact views the video, YouTube will suggest other videos, so they may end up getting a funny cat video that plays after yours. It can't be helped. To avoid this challenge, use the other upload options: Google Drive or a download to your computer. But they seem to take longer than YouTube.

Paperless Post

Deluxe Emails with a Real-Mail Look

paperlesspost.com

My husband proposed to me in August of 2010. After a negative experience with my practice husband, I wasn't about to let this good one get away. So we set the date a mere three months into the future. This gave me no time to get traditional invitations in the mail, so I chose the elegant email service **Paperless Post** to create what I thought were handsome replicas of a paper invitation.

Paperless Post sends emails that look like envelopes and open dramatically when you click. You can send invitations, thank-you notes, birthday cards and all kinds of greetings through these services. You will probably see an uptick in both your open rates and ROI because they're different, fun and interactive. Paperless Post has free and paid options.

Also Check Out...

Although fancy emails are super cool, people still love to get personal notes in the mail. Check out my favorite hard copy options on Page 231.

Manage Calls

We text. We email. We message. We post. And sometimes we even still call. Here are a couple of tools that make your time on the phone a little less annoying.

Start with...

Slydial
Phone Service that Goes Straight to Voicemail
slydial.com

Do you ever dial the phone with a grimace, hoping like heck the recipient doesn't pick up? Use **Slydial** to skip straight to voicemail so you can leave your message and get on with your life. Slydial only works with mobile numbers, but it's super handy. The free version makes you listen to their ad about the premium version, which is only about $30 a year.

Members of my audience told me about Slydial, so it's no surprise that some of my NerdHerders named it as their favorite tool. Clark Jones likes that you can follow up quickly with clients. And Donna Mikesh says, "Slydial Allows you to make a necessary call, leave a message and not get tied up on a call when time is tight."

Then Try...

MeetingMogul
Teleconference Aid that Dials All those Access Codes Automatically
meetingmogulapp.com

Even in this video-heavy world, we still have teleconferences. And even though we have all the answers we need in our ever-present devices, we still fumble to find the passcode and push * when we need to push #.

MeetingMogul transforms the meeting info in your web-based calendar to a one-button click to connect to teleconferences. You'll find all your teleconferences organized in your MeetingMogul agenda, and you can even reach out to other participants via text or email just in case you're running late.

Also Check Out...

Google Voice
Call Management System
voice.google.com

Have you ever had to write an email to someone that says, "If it's after 5 PM, call on this line; or call the office during the weekdays, unless it's Tuesday, when you can reach me at the volunteer center"?

Google Voice gives you one phone number to text, call and check voicemail. You can reach it from any device, managing all your communications in one place wherever you are.

It's not a phone service; let's call it an advanced call-management system. Most of the awesome features are free, and it can centralize (and revolutionize) your phone and text communications. My manager, Molly, uses a Google Voice number for calls to Nerd HQ so she can answer work calls on her personal phone without having to share her real number.

The truth is, I've been worried about Google Voice for several years because they stopped updating it and it seemed forgotten. But in 2016, Google brought new features and energy to the service, and I'm thrilled to recommend it again.

Here's a partial list of Google Voice awesomeness:

- Custom vanity phone numbers
- One number that can route to all your phones
- Free and low-cost national and international calls
- Free text messaging
- Call screening and blocking
- Transcribed voicemails
- Personalized greetings for different incoming numbers
- Conference calls
- Call recording and archiving
- Mobile apps for multiple operating systems

NerdHerd Thumbs Up: HulloMail

HulloMail
Voicemail Management System
hullomail.com

If you're in an industry that receives a lot of calls, check out **HulloMail**. This voicemail management app comes with an enthusiastic recommendation from NerdHerder Chris Christensen. The voicemail-in-the-cloud functionality gives you the ability to save, search and share voicemails, and even receive and catalog the transcriptions with paid upgrades. "HulloMail makes life convenient, and my voicemail box is never full," Chris says.

Send Free Text and Voice Messages

The world is a big place, but technology can make us seem like our far-away friends are right next door. These tools offer free communication across the miles.

Start with...

WhatsApp
Free Text, Phone and Video Messenger
whatsapp.com

WhatsApp's About Us page states that 1 billion people in more than 180 countries use the tool. The premise is pretty basic: WhatsApp gives you free text and voice communications through a secure network. Facebook owns the company, but it's a stand-alone tool for now, even though Facebook Messenger also offers free messaging, as well as audio and video calls. The company claims that its end-to-end encryption equals private communications, though the tool Signal gets generally higher marks in the privacy category.

Then Try...

GroupMe
Group Text Messenger
groupme.com

When you're working with colleagues who no longer answer emails or pick up the phone, **GroupMe** may be the answer. You can set up a group for texting and sharing images, videos and even your location.

GroupMe is cool because other members of the group don't have to download the app to make the system work. Oh, and it's free. NerdHerder David Hayes says, "GroupMe is great for communicating to activity and friend groups (softball team, Sunday school group, etc.) with groups for each." And Ginger Luby adds, "I love connecting with family members… just family, not like Facebook. GroupMe is more intimate, and I've also it for kids' sport teams."

Signal Private Messenger

Secure Private Messenger

whispersystems.org

The messaging app **Signal** made headlines when White House staffers were accused of using the app to secretly leak news to the press. Signal definitely has the best reputation as a private messaging app, although the tool is less known than WhatsApp and other competitors. You can text and call on this system and rest assured that no one can intercept your communication (at least until someone figures out how to do so).

Also Check Out...

Remind

Group Texting Tool for Teachers and More

remind.com

This tool was created for the world of education, but **Remind** has potential for other groups that need to connect via text. Remind asks teachers to set up group texting for designated classes. Students and parents sign up for the class updates, and instructors can send little notes about tomorrow's test or a new resource for homework. Everyone's phone numbers are kept confidential, and teachers can allow two-way conversations to correspond directly with students and parents.

COMMUNICATE

Hot Topic:
Apps to Work Off the Grid

One hacker told the story of spying on the emails of a journalist through in-flight Wi-Fi at 30k feet. This episode (and many like it) just underlines the numerous risks that we take when we log in to public Wi-Fi —even the Wi-Fi we pay for that seems legit.

The problem is that so much of what we do with our phones requires us to be online: social media, maps, messaging. (That's why NerdHerder Linda Whale de Vargas lists her mobile hotspot as her most valuable tech tool). If we're not connected to the grid, we can't function, right?

Well, almost. Here are a handful of convenient apps that you can use even when you're not connected.

Google Maps (Page 149)

HERE (Page 151)

Have you ever lost your signal in an underground garage and couldn't figure out how to get out? Well, maybe that only happens to me, but **Google Maps** and **HERE** can help. Both let you download maps in advance and navigate even when you're offline.

FireChat
Mesh-Based Messaging without Data or Wi-Fi
opengarden.com

Using a concept it calls "mesh networking," **FireChat** lets people bounce signals from device to device to text message when they have no data or Wi-Fi.

Pocket (Page 82)

If you're a news junkie like I am, you get a little frustrated when you're out of reach of the latest headlines. You can save content from a number of sources into **Pocket** to read at your convenience.

Commander Compass

GPS Tool for Off-Road Navigation

happymagenta.com/compass

NerdHerder Timothy Burch likes **Commander Compass**, an Apple app that offers GPS and navigation tools for remote locations. "As a surveyor, Commander Compass helps me figure out where I'm at and which direction to go."

Create Surveys and Polls

· ·

Many of us check the temperature of a topic via social media, but for a true information-gathering exercise, we still need to use survey software. Although one company more or less rules this space, you have other choices.

Start with...

SurveyMonkey
Biggest Online Survey Tool
surveymonkey.com

I think it's safe to say that **SurveyMonkey** is the leader in the online survey field. The company was founded in 1999 and has dominated the market for quite some time, gobbling up rivals and related companies along the way, such as Wufoo, Zoomerang and Precision Polling.

SurveyMonkey has always had a free version, although it's tightened the features over the years. These days, you get 10 questions per survey and up to 100 responses, but you can't download any of the data or do anything fancy such as branching based on answers or extensive data analysis.

If your organization really needs survey software, the upgrade versions of this tool are worth the prices (starting at $25/month). Use the data analysis features to break apart results to look at the data from all sides. The first time I used it for a major benchmarking survey for one of my clients, we had to pay an outside statistician the big bucks to pull the data apart to get to the real trends (OK, it was my dad, but he *is* a statistician). By the time we did the follow-up survey, SurveyMonkey had added so many rich analysis tools that my poor father was out of work.

Then Try...

Typeform
Wizard-Format Online Forms
typeform.com

Most online surveys look pretty basic, but **Typeform** has personality. This wizard-like form filler takes participants through questions one by one in a quirky, friendly format. The pricing and free levels compete with SurveyMonkey, but, well, Typeform is just cuter.

Also Check Out...

Google Forms
Google's Free Survey Tool
google.com/forms

Let me make my opinion clear: I adore **Google Forms**. Within minutes you can create a simple form online and get a link to share. I use it all the time to survey my readers, attendees and anyone else I want to hear from. It's 100% free for as many questions and responses as you want.

So why is this not my first recommendation? Well, it's just plain ugly. It's blocky, simplistic and kinda clunky. It is free and looks free, and it has Google branding at the bottom to tell everyone that it is free. So it's wonderful, but it may be too simple and unprofessional for business needs.

COMMUNICATE

FastField Mobile Forms

Field-Ready Inspection and Checklist Tool

fastfieldforms.com

Chris Champion, a longtime NerdHerder, recently discovered **FastField Mobile Forms**, a handy tool to create inspection sheets, offline forms and other info-gathering surveys you may need on the go. Chris says, "Much more than a survey form, FastField Mobile Forms allow logic to be set up in the form and for customized reporting. It's something new and different I have just discovered, so I am nominating it!"

Nerd HQ Thumbs Up: Cognito Forms

Cognito Forms

Molly's Favorite Form Tool

cognitoforms.com

Molly Gardner, my manager, often sends along standout tech tools for my consideration. And she sent me a short note about **Cognito Forms**: "One of our clients just used this and I like it." I have to agree that Cognito Forms looks awesome. Not only does it have a beefy free version for forms, it also can handle registrations and proposals, including payment options. The paid versions are very reasonable as well.

My Smart Sister's Favorite Tool: Kahoot

Kahoot
Trivia and Quiz Game for Audiences
kahoot.it

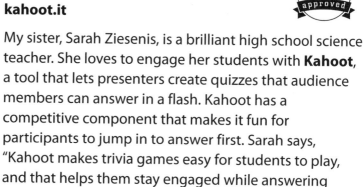

My sister, Sarah Ziesenis, is a brilliant high school science teacher. She loves to engage her students with **Kahoot**, a tool that lets presenters create quizzes that audience members can answer in a flash. Kahoot has a competitive component that makes it fun for participants to jump in to answer first. Sarah says, "Kahoot makes trivia games easy for students to play, and that helps them stay engaged while answering academic questions."

Reference

· ·

I want to . . .

Keep Up with the News

One of the ways to grow your career (and your recipe collection) is to keep up with the latest news and your favorite blogs. These tools bring important topics to you.

Start with...

Flipboard

Magazine-Style Content Aggregator

flipboard.com

Pocket

Saved Article Library for Online and Offline Reading

getpocket.com

Flipboard is a content curating platform that lets you combine your favorite topics and news sources into a beautiful, easy-to-access custom magazine. Once you choose topics to follow, you can save your favorite articles into **Pocket** or a personal channel on Flipboard. I created a board called Nerdy News where I collect and share my favorite tech content. When I need ideas for the blog or NerdWords newsletter, I go back through my archives to find the ideas I saved.

NerdHerder Stuart Sweeney adds, "Flipboard is great. It consolidates news feeds and special interest topics, and you just flip the pages."

Pocket allows you to tuck any article or website into a virtual folder to read later from anywhere: Nooks, Android devices, iOS devices, desktops and other devices. You'll find options to save to Pocket on many major sites and readers, allowing you to instantly add articles and pages to your account to read anywhere. A completely useable version of Pocket is free, but the company has a premium level as well.

Then Try...

Feedly
RSS Feed Aggregator
feedly.com

> *My attorney husband came home from a law*   #NerdFail
> *conference going on and on about a service that*
> *would let him collect interesting articles about bankruptcy and share*
> *them on social media. "It's called 'Freely,'" he said proudly. "Haven't*
> *you heard of it?"*
>
> *Ummm, yeah, honey. I've heard of it. But it's "**Feedly**." Poor guy.*
> *He's yet to earn his nerd cred.*

Feedly lets you pull the RSS feeds from any news source or blog and weave them together into your own news site. Then you can share news, keep articles and aggregate the content you want to know about. Feedly became the best replacement for the popular but now deceased Google Reader.

The Skimm
News at a Glance
theskimm.com

Several audience members tell me they love the news updates from **The Skimm**, which picks out the best headlines for your inbox every day.

Pulse
LinkedIn's Curated News Feed
linkedin.com/pulse

LinkedIn Pulse aggregates the articles from your connections as well as editor's choice topics into one list to help you understand what your professional community cares about. The topics are solid, but the service doesn't have easy ways to save your content for later reading or viewing like Flipboard and Pocket.

Translate Anything

• •

In Star Trek, intergalactic travelers used the Universal Translator gadget to communicate with Klingons and other beings that didn't speak the Federation Standard language (which happened to be English—lucky for us).

Today's translation technology represents science fiction come to life. It is a good time to be a nerd.

Start with...

Microsoft Translator
Translation Tool with Instant Translation
   for Multiple Languages
translator.microsoft.com

An American, a German and a Russian walk into a bar.

The American says, "Let's all be friends. I'll buy the next round!"

The German and the Russian smile awkwardly and go back to their phones. They don't speak English, so… awkward.

But then the German yells out a happy "Ich habe eine Idee!" and starts pointing to an app on his phone. He gestures for everyone to download **Microsoft Translator**, and within seconds, the three are all using the instant translation feature. The German repeats again, "Ich habe eine Idee!" and the American and Russian cheer because his words, "I have an idea!" are now instantly translated on their phones.

Microsoft Translator has been around for a while, but recently they made game-changing improvements that will help all of us immediately. Nerdy tech folks call this technology "deep learning" and "neural networks," but they're just making those terms up. It just means that technology is becoming smarter than we are.

The conversation feature lets someone set up a "room" for chatting. You just put your first name and choose the language you speak. Some languages (such as English, Russian, Spanish, Chinese, Arabic and more) offer the instant speech-to-text translations, and many others that will translate text. To interact, you press the microphone and start talking. Up to 100 colleagues can see what you're saying instantly translated on their screens and respond in their own languages, which will be translated on your device.

NerdHerder Jim Petersen nominated it as his favorite tool just from my recommendation. "I've never actually had a chance to use it... Beth Z just told me about it. But it sounds really cool."

Then Try...

Google Translate

Translation Tool with Augmented Reality Tools
translate.google.com and **in App Stores**

Just like Microsoft, **Google Translate** can handle audio and written translation jobs. But Google's best party trick is its use of augmented reality on printed material. The mobile app lets you scan words and watch them magically transform to another language in real time on your screen. The feature will help you read menus at exotic restaurants.

Also Check Out...

TextGrabber   #NerdPartyTrick

Translator App with OCR
textgrabber.pro

Abbyy, the maker of FineScanner (Page 111), uses its exceptional OCR tools in **TextGrabber** to digitize printed material and translate them instantly. What's more, the work happens without an internet connection.

Learn a New Language

Poor Rosetta Stone. The language-learning software has found major competition with free options. This is wonderful for all of us, but horrible for my stock portfolio (I bought Rosetta Stone stock before the free apps caught on).

Start with...

Duolingo
Gamified Free Language-Learning System
duolingo.com

Duolingo has changed the way people learn languages. Instead of listening to language tapes in your car during a commute, you can listen to mini-lessons with games and tricks to keep you engaged and encouraged. You get points for completing lessons multiple days in a row and hearts when you get answers correct. Your progress is synched between your app and the web, so you can sneak in a lesson anywhere. It's 100% free and doesn't even make you navigate through ads to learn dozens of languages. (Stay tuned for the Klingon class!)

Then Try...

Tandem
Language Practice App
tandem.net

Now that you've learned the basics of a new language with Duolingo, you need to find a practice partner. **Tandem** is a community of language learners who help each other practice and learn. Like Duolingo, Tandem is free.

Also Check Out...

ELSA

English Pronunciation Assistance
elsanow.io

English has its quirks and challenges, and non-native speakers (or people with heavy accents) can be at a disadvantage in the workplace. The **ELSA** app gently corrects your pronunciation of English words and helps you feel more comfortable and confident speaking in English.

Use Study Aids

•••

Need to study for a professional certification or even help your kids with math homework? There's an app for that.

Start with...

Photomath
App that Solves Math Problems with a Click
photomath.net

If you never used flashcards to learn your multiplication tables, you may need a little help with your kid's math homework. **Photomath** uses your mobile camera to solve math problems in real time, and will even take you step-by-step through the solution. Parents tell me it's easy to snap a picture of a math problem when your kid steps away from his homework for a bathroom break. Then when your little math genius returns, you're suddenly empowered with the answer, just like you knew what you were doing all along.

Then Try...

Anki
Flashcards to Study Wherever You Go
ankisrs.net

Cram
Another Flashcard App
cram.com

TinyCards
Duolingo Flashcard App
tinycards.duolingo.com

The guy who won the most in a single day on the game show *Jeopardy!* supposedly used the **Anki** flashcard system to prep for the show. Anki lets you set up decks of flashcards that you can use to study anywhere. You can find a whole host of tools at **ankisrs.net** or try the apps at **ankiapp.com**. **Cram's** apps also come recommended by attendees from my sessions. And we were all happy when language-learning Duolingo (Page 86) released **TinyCards** for language flashcards and more. All three resources have free and paid versions.

Also Check Out...

Primer
Quick Sales and Marketing Training
yourprimer.com

Sometimes we need a little more education about fundamental business tips. Even if we're in the back office at our organization, we're a part of the sales team for our company. **Primer** shares little lessons and activities from Google about marketing and more—a little education for everyone on your team.

NerdHerd Thumbs Up:
Legal Research

Justia
Law Research Site
law.justia.com/cases

James B. Martin appreciates the legal resources at **Justia** because "I can find research information on any pending, current or previous law cases."

Check the Weather

All the weather apps out there probably rely on the same data sources to provide the forecasts, but the way they present the info is as varied as snowflakes.

Start with...

Dark Sky
Unnervingly Precise Weather App
darksky.net

Dark Sky describes itself as a "hyperlocal" weather app, specializing in micro-forecasts for the two-foot square that surrounds you and your phone. I was walking around on a warm afternoon in Florida when I downloaded it. The forecast predicted a light downpour starting in 4 minutes and lasting for 7 minutes followed by clear skies. Sure enough, I had just enough time to duck under an overhang before the rain came down. And it lasted almost exactly 7 minutes. Not all the predictions have been that accurate, but it's a beautiful, simple, useable resource that has become my favorite weather app.

Then Try...

What the Forecast?!!
Weather Forecasts with Giggles
nightcatproductions.com/whattheforecast

Weather Underground
Best Overall Weather App
wunderground.com

WunderMap

Online Weather Tracker from Weather Underground
wunderground.com/wundermap

With daily weather facts such as, "It's a great day for naps. Followed by naps," **What the Forecast?!!** is not really safe for work but is oh so funny. And it happens to be darn accurate, too.

Weather Underground's resources always show up on "best of" lists for accuracy, clarity and ease of use. Whether you visit the site, play with the interactive **WunderMap** or download the apps, you can be assured you're getting the most accurate info from the best sources. (But it won't be funny.)

Also Check Out...

Storm

Weather Underground's Storm-Tracking App
wunderground.com/storm

Weather Underground's specialty app **Storm** helps you track severe weather patterns, gives you alerts and keeps you up to date on dangerous situations.

REFERENCE

Improve My Writing

•••

As a writer, I'm verbose… too casual with a propensity to write sentences that go on and on and on. My husband might say that describes my speaking style as well, but I've never run my speeches through these writing analysis tools to help me improve.

Don't be like me. Use these writing tools.

Start with...

Hemingway App
Online Writing Editor
hemingwayapp.com

People are so clever and helpful, especially when they're trying to make you more clever and helpful. The online app called **Hemingway** lets you paste or write text on the page, and with one button click, the system analyzes your words and sentence structure to give you tips for clearer, more concise writing.

Hemingway (which is free, of course) gives you a Readability Grade that corresponds to how educated your audience needs to be to get the point. The system recommends you write for Grade 10—not because your readers might not have graduated from high school—but because your message may come out more clearly when you cut down on the verbiage and get to the point.

Hemingway pushes you to eliminate adverbs and passive voice, plus it helps you shrink your sentences and avoid run-on messes. The system color codes your text to show you the problems.

Then Try...

PaperRater
Online Writing Editor with Option for Paper Submissions
paperrater.com

Like the Hemingway App, **PaperRater** evaluates text you paste or upload to check for common grammar and spelling mistakes, as well as style. It also gives you an official grade. I don't place much stock in their grading scale because the system just gave my writing sample a C. I don't get Cs.

One characteristic that stands out with PaperRater is the feature that allows teachers to create a code to collect submissions. Students can check their work then submit their papers to their teachers, and the system will automatically scan the submission for plagiarism—a deluxe feature that PaperRater gives to schools for free.

Also Check Out...

Ginger Page
Writing Help for Your Mobile Device
gingersoftware.com

You can check writing online with **Ginger Page**, but the best feature is the mobile app. Write or dictate a text message into the app to strengthen UR communication skills and avoid awkward abbreviations and text shorthand. (Heh. See what I did there?)

Grammarly
English Teacher on Your Laptop
grammarly.com

If you miss the days when your English teacher peered over your shoulder as you wrote, you'll like **Grammarly**. Download the Chrome plugin or the software for your computer, and the system will monitor what you write in real time. It's a helpful tool, but the free version finds "advanced" errors that it won't disclose unless you upgrade.

Organize Citations for Online Research

• •

The first time I wrote a paper that required footnotes and a bibliography, I had to type it on a typewriter and count the number of lines to leave at the bottom to leave space for the notes. And about a decade after that when I wrote my master's thesis, I kept track of my bibliography on handwritten index cards.

Boy, do kids today have it easy with these methods to organize bibliographies (insert Gen X sigh).

Start with...

Mendeley
Research and Bibliography Tool with Mobile Apps
mendeley.com

Zotero
Research and Bibliography Tool
zotero.com

Mendeley and **Zotero** can take a good deal of the pain out of maintaining a bibliography and tracking citations in any researched report. Use the Zotero browser add-on to grab citations straight from the web. You can also add references manually or use the stand-alone desktop tool. Mendeley gives you similar downloadables plus mobile apps. You can also use both tools to save PDFs and other documents for searching and annotation. The new technology sure beats the printouts and highlighters I used to use (still bitter).

Then Try...

PaperShip
iOS App for Mendeley and Zotero
papershipapp.com

Though Zotero doesn't have its own app, you can use **PaperShip** to collect and annotate PDFs, articles and other notes on your iPhone or iPad. The app connects to both Zotero and Mendeley.

Also Check Out...

As much as I like the third-party citation tools, you don't have to go outside your word processing tools to manage a bibliography. Both Microsoft and Google G Suite have internal bibliography and citation tools. Microsoft has also improved its writing and spelling review capabilities, giving the other reference tools a little free competition.

REFERENCE

Discover New Apps and Tools

Wanna be nerdy like me? Here are some of my favorite ways to keep up with the latest apps and tech tools.

Start with...

Product Hunt
The Ultimate Source for New Technology
producthunt.com

Every time CNN talks about a hot new app, you can bet that **Product Hunt** had the scoop first. Based on the Reddit concept where people post ideas and other readers vote up the best ones, Product Hunt members share new app discoveries with the community, and the most popular tools bubble to the top every day.

I use both the app and the site to stay on top of the latest technology, books, podcasts and other products. I use IFTTT (Page 156) to create a recipe: When I upvote a tool on Product Hunt, IFTTT saves it into a Google spreadsheet. At last count, the spreadsheet has more than 1200 saved tools, at least 100 of which are in this book.

Then Try...

AppAdvice Apps Gone Free
Best iOS Apps Gone Free Every Day
appadvice.com/apps-gone-free

AppGratis
One Free App Every Day
appgratis.com

You can find several tools like **Apps Gone Free** and **AppGratis**, but these are two of the best. The concept is that each day they report on paid apps that are free for a limited time. Download the app while it's free, then delete it if you don't need it right away. When you restore it later, you still won't have to pay.

Apple got its nose out of joint about these types of apps in 2013 and removed them from the App Store, but AppGratis and a few others are available for Android. You can also just visit the sites.

Hot Topic:
How Do You Know If a New
App Is Safe to Download?

I have a few guidelines to protect myself from malware, bad apps and other infected technology.

- I research whatever I find on reputable sites like the ones in this section. If a tool seems too obscure or unknown, I'll wait until it has a little more web history.

- I use safeguards to protect my identity like the ones on Page 122 to not sign up for new things unless I'm sure that they're safe.

- I am very careful about the place I download a tool. Apple's App Store has very rigorous requirements for app approval, so apps from there are *rarely* inherently evil. Android is a different story. Be super, super, super careful about installing any Android app from outside the Google Play Store—and use common sense about apps within the store as well.

Also Check Out...

These are some of the sites I follow on Flipboard (Page 82) to keep up with tech news.

Lifehacker
lifehacker.com

Mashable
mashable.com

TechCrunch
techcrunch.com

And check out a recommendation from NerdHerd member Richard Wright.

Kim Komando
Tech Tool Guru
komando.com

Richard gets tech tips, breaking news and security alerts from **Kim Komando**. "Komando is a great resource for immediate security info, technical advice and current happenings in the tech world. I have followed her for many years."

Utilities

• •

I want to . . .

Capture Info from Computer Screens

Every once in a while, you need to capture a picture or video of what you're seeing on a screen. Both Windows and Mac operating systems have built-in screencapture tools, but the tools in this section add extra features that you may find you can't live without.

Start with...

Jing and/or Snagit

The Best Screencapture Tools

techsmith.com

One of my favorite free tools of all time is **Jing**, a download from TechSmith. Jing sits on the edge of your screen in the form of a little yellow sun. Click the capture button, and the crosshairs tool gives you the ability to highlight a portion of the screen. Then capture a picture of the screen to annotate (a screenshot) or start a movie that captures your voice and every movement on the screen (a screencast).

The beauty of Jing is that it can take just seconds to grab a screenshot, draw some arrows, write a note then click a button to copy or share the image… ditto with the video capture after you demo something on the screen, with a narration, if you like.

If you own Jing's big brother, **Snagit** ($50), you can choose to edit your capture with Snagit's advanced editing tools such as borders and stamps and a blur tool to obscure private information. You can also capture scrolling screens with Snagit. Although Snagit is the paid option, I use Jing much more often because it's so easy to share. And it's cuter.

Then Try...

Screencast-O-Matic
Browser-Based Screen Recorder
screencastomatic.com

Screencastify
Another Browser-Based Screen Recorder
screencastify.com

Recording your screen with either of these tools could hardly be easier. For **Screencast-O-Matic**, just go to the site and launch the recorder—no registration needed. **Screencastify** has a browser plugin that you can click from any tab. Both let you record and narrate what's happening on your screen, with or without a webcam. They both have very modestly priced pro versions and robust free versions. The biggest difference is that Screencastify records video in a web-specific format that you'll have to convert if you want to use it in a video editor. Screencast-O-Matic offers more traditional video formats. And it has the coolest name.

UTILITIES

Also Check Out...

Reflector
Screen Mirroring Tool for Your Mobile Devices
airsquirrels.com/reflector

If you need to capture a video demo from something on your mobile device, you'll love the **Reflector App**. Reflector enables you to mirror your mobile screen on your computer, where you can record your movements and capture a voiceover as well.

Create and Edit PDFs

• •

Adobe developed the Portable Document Format (PDF) in the early 1990s as a common document format that would allow fonts, pictures, formatting and styles to be locked into any type of file so that every recipient would see it the same way.

There are now a kabillion (approximately) different free and bargain sites, software packages and apps that compete directly with Adobe. I'm not even going to attempt to give a full list of PDF tools. You can find them as cloud-based sites, stand-alone downloads, browser plug-ins and mobile apps. But here are a few major players I use and respect.

Start with...

Adobe Reader
The Original PDF Tool
get.adobe.com/reader

If you haven't taken a close look at your regular old **Adobe Reader**, you are missing out.

Many of the features that used to be only in the paid version are free now. You can add notes to documents, cross out and replace text, fill out forms, and track changes from multiple editors. You can even add audio notes and a stamp.

The coolest feature of Reader is the ability to sign a document. No more printing out a PDF, signing it, then scanning it back in and attaching it to an email. Now you can just load your signature into the program, then click and paste it where you want it. To load your signature, you can either upload a scan of your signature, sign on a trackpad or use a built-in stylized signature in Reader.

Note: Adobe Reader will really try hard to get you to send your document for a signature—and sign up for their paid service to do it. If you don't need extensive tracking options, ignore those pop-ups and buttons. Simply save the signed PDF as a separate file and send it as an attachment.

Then Try...

Foxit Reader

Windows Adobe Reader Alternative
foxitsoftware.com/products/pdf-reader

Foxit Reader might be the best Adobe Reader replacement for Windows. You can annotate, fill forms and protect yourself from malicious PDFs with the Trust Manager mode. The ConnectedPDF feature lets you collaborate on PDFs with others. Plus, Foxit will let you publish and scan documents into PDF format and even embed images and videos.

Also Check Out...

Adobe Fill & Sign

Adobe's PDF Form Filler
In App Stores

Both Adobe and Foxit have mobile apps that kick you-know-what. They are good for reading and annotating PDFs on the go.

Even better for PDF management on the go is **Adobe Fill & Sign**. This tool, ummm, lets you fill and sign. My attendees love it.

Type More Efficiently

• •

It almost seems trivial to review keyboard apps. I mean, typing is typing, right? QWERTY is spelled the same everywhere you look. But finding a keyboard that matches your typing style and communication needs can dramatically improve your productivity.

Start with...

Fleksy
Custom Mobile Keyboard with Super-Smart Predictive Text
fleksy.com

SwiftKey
Custom Mobile Keyboard with Swipe Typing
swiftkey.com

Swype
Another Custom Mobile Keyboard with Swipe Typing
swype.com

Third-party keyboards can drastically improve your typing efficiency on mobile devices. From the advanced predictive typing capabilities of **Fleksy** to the swipe-to-type features of **SwiftKey** and **Swype**, these apps are designed to help you avoid an awkward hunt-and-peck typing experience.

The main difference between Fleksy and the other two is that Fleksy is supposed to be better at predictive text but doesn't have the swiping feature. Fleksy also has a cool space bar tool that lets you more easily scroll backwards or forwards through text without having to stick your finger on the right line of text. Here are other key features of these third-party keyboards:

- Customizability
- Faster typing
- Predictive text
- GIF and emoji integration

Then Try...

Gboard
Google's Custom Mobile Keyboard
In App Stores

Word Flow Keyboard
Microsoft's Mobile Keyboard with One-Handed Typing
In App Stores

Google and Microsoft are bringing their rivalry to every keystroke. Both companies released mobile keyboards to make typing, searching and communicating faster and easier on mobile devices.

Both **Gboard** and **Word Flow** include swipe-to-type features like Swype and SwiftKey, but they also include built-in internet search capabilities as well as the very handy capacity to find the perfect GIF.

You can personalize the keyboard with different colors or backgrounds, but Word Flow is definitely the prettier of the two. Word Flow's biggest distinction from Gboard is a twisting keyboard that makes it easier to type with one hand.

UTILITIES

Also Check Out...

TextExpander

Text Expansion Tool for Computers and Mobile Devices (Kind of)

textexpander.com

When you type "teh" in Microsoft Word, the software automatically converts it to "the." **TextExpander** lets you set up tons of autocorrects and text shortcuts to make your typing quicker and more efficient no matter where you are typing. Create shortcuts for inserting the date, your signature, addresses, common replies and much more. You can download the software on Windows and Mac machines, and apps will bring your shortcuts to mobile devices. In 2016, TextExpander made the world mad by switching to a subscription price model, but you can still get a free trial.

Convert Almost Anything

Let's say you're working with an incredible graphic designer. He sends you the first draft of the incredibly important graphic you've commissioned—a graphic you have to unveil at a meeting you're having in three minutes. You click on this file, knowing you're about to see a masterpiece; and then a frustrating pop-up announces, "Windows cannot open this file. What do you want to do?"

Don't waste a moment of your precious time trying to fight with a file that won't open. Here are a few tools to help you identify random files and convert on the go.

Start with...

Zamzar

File Converter Extraordinaire
zamzar.com

Zamzar has saved my hide multiple times. Simply visit the site, upload a file, choose what you want to turn it into and press a button. In a matter of minutes, your file is transformed into the format you need.

Wait, there's more! You can convert files via email as well, just by writing to [format]@zamzar.com. For example, you can send your Microsoft Word file to pdf@zamzar.com. In a few minutes, you'll receive a link to your new pdf. Or you can send your PDF to doc@zamzar.com, and the opposite happens. It's magic either way.

Then Try...

FileInfo

Reference Site to Identify File Extensions

fileinfo.com

When extensions look suspicious, I head over to **FileInfo** to check them out before clicking. The site is kept up to date with every possible file extension. You can search by file type (audio, game, executables, etc.) or simply enter the extension into the search engine. After you know what you're dealing with, the site gives you a list of applications that will open it.

Also Check Out...

WolframAlpha

Where All the Knowledge in the World Lives

wolframalpha.com

It's impossible to exaggerate the wealth of knowledge you'll find on **WolframAlpha**, which calls itself a "Computational Knowledge Engine." You can convert measurements, analyze data, look up IP addresses, compare the statistics of The Beatles' White Album to Jay Z's The Black Album, get step-by-step instructions for a physics calculation... I mean. Wow. From the about page:

> *Our goal is to accept completely free-form input, and to serve as a knowledge engine that generates powerful results and presents them with maximum clarity.*

> *We aim to collect and curate all objective data; implement every known model, method, and algorithm; and make it possible to compute whatever can be computed about anything.*

NerdHerd Thumbs Up: Measure a Room

My Measures

Tool to Record Measurements of Rooms and Objects

mymeasuresapp.com

NerdHerder Big Papa Von Kaenel (you read that correctly) likes **My Measures**, an app that lets you take a picture of a room or object and add dimensions. "It allows me to visit a project site, take pictures and put the measurements right on the picture," Big Papa says. "My Measures makes it easier to remember the site as well."

UTILITIES

Scan Documents

• •

Gone are the days when scanning a hard-copy document required a scanner. You have many choices of tools to snap a picture of documents and transform them instantly into PDFs and more.

Start with...

Office Lens
Scanning App with OCR Functionality
microsoft.com/officelens

Adobe Scan
Adobe's Text Recognition Tool
acrobat.adobe.com/us/en/acrobat/mobile-app/
   scan-documents.html

Office Lens is a free, simple scanning tool with a hidden game changer. Like many scanners, you can snap a picture of hard-copy documents to turn them into PDFs or images. The secret sauce comes in with your subscription to Microsoft Office 365, which starts at about $69 a year. When you have the subscription, Office Lens lets you snap a picture of a document and immediately edit in Microsoft Word. No hassle. No fuss. Just snap, process, upload and edit.

In May of 2017, **Adobe Scan** jumped into the text-recognition scanner pool. Like Office Lens, you can scan a document to grab the text and use it elsewhere. You'll have to pay for Adobe services to get all the features, but isn't that always the case?

Then Try...

Scanbot
Great Free Scanner
scanbot.io

Genius Scan
Robust Smart Scanning Tool
thegrizzlylabs.com/genius-scan

Maybe it's just the cuteness of the name, but I just love **Scanbot**. This little app is fast, easy and effective for making PDFs and image files of your hard-copy documents. You can upgrade for OCR. But it sucks. So don't.

Genius Scan is equally as popular, just as easy to use and exactly the same amount of free.

Also Check Out...

Abbyy FineScanner
Deluxe Scanner with OCR
finescanner.com

In a line-by-line comparison of an OCR scan, **FineScanner** does a little better than Office Lens, but I've always found Abbyy products to be more expensive than a casual user might need to pay. One special feature is the BookScan option that captures two facing pages separately. With Abbyy products you have plenty of apps and tools in their product line to choose the right scanner for your needs, including one that scans and translates simultaneously.

UTILITIES

Prizmo Go

Scan-and-Paste Text Scanner

creaceed.com

Sometimes you just want to grab a paragraph or two off a hard copy and send it on to a team member. **Prizmo Go** (iOS only for now) scans over text to absorb the clip and send it to a colleague without having to take a fuzzy picture or take a full scan.

NerdHerd Thumbs Up:
More Favorite Scanners

CamScanner

NerdHerd Favorite Scanning Tool

camscanner.com

No less than three NerdHerders mentioned **CamScanner** as their favorite tool. Duane Washkowiak uses CamScanner to sign PDFs. Tami DuBose uses it to convert images to PDF for printing. "I have vendors send me invoices via text. Converting those pictures to pdf makes printing a clean invoice much nicer than the colored, shadowed image received via text." And Shawn Powelson loves how CamScanner helps her with receipts. "I can upload receipts for my expense report without spending hours scanning and copying at the copier."

Scanner Pro
Apple Scanning Tool with OCR
readdle.com

Another NerdHerd favorite is Readdle's **Scanner Pro**. It works like many scanners and has a very accurate OCR option. Chris Legge says, "I've converted most of my paper to the cloud. Scanner Pro integrates very well with OneDrive, and as such, I was able to create 'workflows' to allow easier uploads for specific documents to various folders. So easy!"

Tiny Scanner
Scanning App with an Identity Crisis
appxy.com/tinyscan

Appxy calls this app both **Tiny Scanner** and TinyScan, but either one is a great app according to NerdHerder Kristina Elizondo.

TurboScan
Another Favorite Scan Tool
turboscanapp.com

Finally in the scanning category, NerdHerder Nancy Sharp gives a thumbs up to **TurboScan** because of the ease of editing and sending scanned documents straight from the phone.

UTILITIES

Improve Battery Life

Many modern devices have low-power modes and battery-saving features, but sometimes that's not enough. I haven't been particularly impressed with battery-saving apps that you download, so here are my best tips for improving your battery life.

Hot Topic:
Nine Tips to Improve Your Battery Life

1. Turn Off Wi-Fi and Bluetooth

Your Wi-Fi is constantly searching for signals. You probably have no intention of connecting to the grocery store's wireless connection when you stop in for milk, but your device is spending energy making sure you have that opportunity. The phone has good intentions—to save data—but it can really drain a battery.

When you leave home to run errands, turn off your Wi-Fi, not only to avoid the battery drain, but also to speed up your connection since your device may connect to known networks without permission and slow your overall speed.

2. Don't Auto-Update Apps

Do you need the latest update to Angry Birds (especially since that game is SO 2014)? Probably not. But your device may be automatically updating your apps behind the scenes, sucking up your energy unless you turn off the background refresh setting.

3. Turn Off Auto-Brightness

Your phone can adjust itself to the brightness in your environment, but it'll cost you some juice.

4. Use Do Not Disturb/Sleep Modes

Ever get a text clink in the middle of the night? Of course you do. But if your phone's sitting on the kitchen table, you're not going to hear it (and even if you do hear it, chances are the news can wait). You can set your device to sleep while you're sleeping and save battery life.

5. Turn Off Location Features

When your device is tracking your location, it's working hard. You may not need for Google to know where you are at all times, so turn the master switch off when you're concerned about your battery, and take a hard look at the list of apps that have access to your location.

6. Watch Your Push Technology

Not only are you more easily distracted when your phone is constantly dinging and pinging and notifying you of new baby pictures from Facebook friends, you're also using more battery. Turn off the notifications for email and manage the other pop-up distractions through your settings.

7. Cut Down on Special Effects

Isn't it cool when your background looks animated, or when you can wave a hand to make things happen? Sure, if you're willing to give up some of your battery for a whiz bang experience.

UTILITIES

8. Autolock in Less Time

Sometimes it's annoying when your phone locks up in 2 minutes, but if you set the autolock to put your phone to sleep in shorter intervals, the battery lasts longer.

9. Use Airplane Mode

Airplane mode is not just for airplanes. The setting stops your automatic battery drainers, such as Wi-Fi, Bluetooth, app refresh and more. If you switch your device to airplane mode while it's charging, it juices up much faster (but you can't be playing Angry Birds or fooling with other areas of your phone because it negates the slight advantage).

• •

Security Tools

I want to . . .

SECURITY

Monitor My Family

• •

My wonderful husband is a crazy Ironman   #CreepyButHelpful
triathlete-turned avid camper, and he's
frequently on all-day bike rides or multi-hour
hikes. When I haven't heard from him in a while, my worry gene
kicks in. So, I use the Find iPhone app to track him down.

If you have more people to keep track of, the parents in my sessions
have recommended these apps and tools.

Start with...

Life360
Family Location and Communication System
life360.com

Life360 eliminates the text messages that ask, "Are you there yet?"
Once you set up your "circles," you can view family members on a
map, send messages and receive alerts when they arrive at home,
school or work. Parents in my sessions love being able to rest easy
knowing everyone is safe and sound. New and premium features
include crash alerts, stolen phone protection and round-the-clock
access to a live person for emergency help as well as roadside assistance (like a family-oriented OnStar with a side of AAA).

NerdHerder Heather Hill loves Life360. "I know when my middle
schooler leaves school and arrives home safely."

Then Try...

Glympse
Simple Location Sharer
glympse.com

If you're a worrywart and want to ~~stalk~~ track your loved ones,
Glympse is a fast, free app that shares your location. You can share

your location for a set amount of time, alert people of your travel plans and set up a group to track everyone. People can ~~stalk~~ track each other through the apps or online.

Also Check Out...

You're Done
Phone Control App for Your Kids
youredoneapp.com

A famous speaker colleague of mine, Patrick Henry (Page x), created an app that punishes kids by bricking their cellphones until they learn a lesson. **You're Done** is a genius step for 21st Century parenting, and Patrick's description of the app is hilarious even if you don't have kids. Advice from Patrick...

> *Kids are smart and may find a way to monkey with the functionality of the app. I simply tell my kids "if you disable the app, you lose your phone... and Christmas is canceled."*

NerdHerd Thumbs Up: Game Changer

GameChanger
Sports Tracker for Parents and Grandparents
gc.com

In early 2017, attendees started telling me about their favorite family app, **GameChanger**. The app lets parents, grandparents and faraway aunts follow kids' baseball and basketball games. The coach sets up the app for the team, and family members follow the plays no matter how far away they are from the action. NerdHerder Lori Palermo loves it because, "We get to 'watch' the nephew's away games."

SECURITY

Protect Computer and Mobile Devices

The people who write the warning pop-ups for the built-in security programs should get Pulitzers because they are incredibly effective. Who can resist a note like this?

> *"STOP! If you don't install our full version of this software, your computer will be unprotected and will soon be seething with horrible worms and Trojans!"*

It's easy to give in to the panic and spend another $40+ a year to pay for an antivirus program for your computer, but we don't have to pay a ton of money to protect our investments.

Start with...

Avast Free Antivirus
Feature-Rich Antivirus Tool with Password Management
avast.com

AVG AntiVirus FREE
Essential Antivirus Protection
avg.com

Although **Avast** and **AVG** are still separate entities, Avast bought the other company in 2016. Both have been around for a long time and are some of the best tools out there for antivirus. The two guard against malware, viruses and other bad-people techniques for stealing your data or messing up your life. Both offer software/apps for PCs, Macs and Android devices, and Avast adds an app for iOS.

Then Try...

Malwarebytes

Malware Finder with Anti-Ransomware Updates

malwarebytes.com

Bitdefender Antivirus Free Edition

Antivirus Tool with Great Malware Removal Tools

bitdefender.com

Malware is software such as viruses, worms, Trojan horses and spyware. Isn't it disgusting that we have that many words for the horrible things that bad guys dream up to muck up our computers? Jeeze. **Malwarebytes** has been the best free tool in this category for years. It's the one I use. I like that you can upgrade to get robust protection from ransomware, the programs that literally hold your files hostage and make you pay to get them back. **Bitdefender** also gets great marks.

SECURITY

Stay Safe Online

Hackers have come up with an insane number of ways to dupe you, from phishing emails that make it look like your aunt really is lost in London without money or ID, to sneaky password-stealing fake sites that look exactly like the real thing. These tools can help you take a bite out of cybercrimes.

Start with...

Authenticators

Password Supplement Security Tools

Google, Microsoft, LastPass and other companies have created **authenticators** to help with password security. They generate one-time-use codes that you need to input in addition to your username and password every time you log in to applications that allow the extra service. The authenticator is on your phone. When you want to log in to a site that uses two-factor authentication, you provide your username and password then run the authenticator app. The app displays a code and transmits to the site, which then asks you to input it to proceed.

Google, Microsoft and LastPass (Page 126) all offer authenticators, as do other companies.

Then Try...

EmailOnDeck
Free Temporary Email Addresses
emailondeck.com

Mailinator
Instant @mailinator.com Email Inboxes
mailinator.com

Both **EmailOnDeck** and **Mailinator** work to stop spammers from collecting your contact info in the first place. EmailOnDeck's home page generates a one-time-use email address that you can plug into a registration site to download a great whitepaper or what-have-you. If the site requires you verify your email address or sends the download to your inbox, your EmailOnDeck address is good for a small period of time so you can retrieve your mail.

Mailinator lets you create an email address on the fly with this formula: [anything]@mailinator.com. The inbox for your made-up address is already up and running at malinator.com. Just put in your [anything], and all the mail for that address shows up. Note: Unlike EmailOnDeck, every email on Mailinator (in the free version at least) is public. They make their policy clear in the FAQs:

> *Question: This sounds pretty insecure. What if I want to send important emails with sensitive super-secret information in them to Mailinator?*

> *Answer: Then you are a stupid-head. That isn't what this is for.*

Interestingly enough, Mailinator played an unwitting role in a 2017 worldwide phishing attack that used an app that mimicked a Google Docs share from a colleague. The bad guy set up hhhhhhhhhh@mailinator.com as a phony email and wreaked havoc on millions in less than an hour.

Search Better and Faster

• •

Ever hear someone say, "Let me *Bing* that for you"? Probably not. Google dominates the world of search engines with almost 80% of the market. Although it's arguably the best tool, other search engines may help you find what you need more quickly and more securely.

Start with...

DuckDuckGo

Search Engine with Privacy Protection

duckduckgo.com

Besides having the most adorable name, **DuckDuckGo** has the reputation of being the most private. When you search using DuckDuckGo, your history isn't tracked or sold to advertisers.

Then Try...

Dogpile

Search Results of Multiple Search Engines

dogpile.com

Different search engines will return different results for the same search. **Dogpile** runs your inquiry on multiple search engines at once, then ranks the results for relevance and eliminates duplicates.

Also Check Out...

Wayback Machine

Search Engine for the Past

archive.org/web

On the web, nothing really disappears. The **Wayback Machine** is the archive of the internet. It has been taking snapshots of publicly available sites since 1996. Just put the site into the search engine, and you can click back in time to see the site on different dates.

And Don't Forget...

Google
The World's Most Popular Search Engine
google.com

NerdHerder Cindy Cara adds a reminder of the awesomeness that is the **Google** search engine. "Google gives me access, through detailed searching, to all of the knowledge in the world. Past and present! I can find out anything I want to know and can find people and communicate with them directly about what they know and what they do."

SECURITY

Hot Topic:
How Can I Improve My Search Results?

Most of us stop at the first page of search results and get frustrated when we don't find what we need right away. Here are a few search tips for any search engine that can greatly improve your results.

- Put quotes around a word or phrase to get the exact match.
- Use an asterisk as a wildcard, such as "tallest * in the U.S."
- Use the minus sign to exclude words from your search, such as "famous nerds –geeks"
- Use *AND* and *OR* between words and phrases to expand or restrict your search.
- Drag an image into the search bar on the Google Images page to search by image.
- Use the microphone in the search bar to search by voice.
- Bonus! If you want to search Google in ridiculous ways, check out **elgoog.im**.

Manage Passwords

One of the most common online security mistakes we make, besides picking passwords that are too easy, is using the same password for multiple sites.

The bad guys know this, and when they hack into a site, they get our username/password combos and try them on other sites and eventually get to some pretty valuable information. It's time to truly take charge of your password and internet security issues.

Start with...

LastPass

One of the Top Five Password Managers

lastpass.com

LastPass is a password manager that lets you generate unique, very complicated passwords for every site you visit then makes them accessible so you never have to remember them.

After an unnervingly quick search, LastPass discovers all the usernames and passwords you've ever used on your computer and stores them in a vault. You access your entries via one giant password—the last password you'll ever need. (LastPass—get it?) When you visit a page while you're logged into LastPass via browser plug-ins, the tool will fill in your username/password automatically.

I use LastPass over the other top password managers for a few reasons. The biggest factor is probably that I tried LastPass first, and once everything was set up, I was too lazy to change. Also, I've been pleased with their responsiveness to major security challenges, including their solid response after a fierce hack attack in 2015. A couple of other reasons: LastPass makes it very easy to share passwords with people; the premium version is insanely cheap; and the regular improvements have made it increasingly easy to use.

NerdHerders LOVE LastPass. Vickie Lester gives it a thumbs up. Carol Hamilton likes that it helps her use better passwords on the sites she visits. And Joyce Pleva says, "LastPass makes my life easier because everything is in one place."

Then Try...

You can't really go wrong with any of the top password managers. Here's a quick list of the best and their unique features.

KeePass

Open-Source Password Manager with Local Storage
keepass.info

KeePass is an open-source program that you download or store on a USB drive. KeePass stores all your information locally by default, so if you're worried about the security of the cloud, this could be an option. It was built for Windows, but there are ways to use it on other platforms. I can't bring myself to use KeePass because it seems to be one "p" short of a socially acceptable name: I keep reading it as "Keep-ass." That's just wrong.

1Password

Top Password Manager with Offline Storage and Manual Sync
agilebits.com/onepassword

Unlike the other password managers on this list, **1Password** doesn't have a free version. You pay per device, per user and per version. But the price is a one-time purchase, so you'll probably save money in the long run.

Like KeePass, 1Password stores your passwords offline, but you can sync to other devices over USB or Wi-Fi, or online with a cloud-based service like Dropbox (Page 14) or iCloud. Oh, and the best new feature? Check out the Travel Mode, which removes your password vault from your device when you're traveling, so if an official searches your device, your private info won't show up (and won't even look like it was ever there).

SECURITY

NerdHerd Favorite Password Tools

Several members of the NerdHerd have their favorite password management tools. And they're smart folks, so check them out. ☺

Dashlane

Top Password Manager with Online/
Offline Storage Options

dashlane.com

If I hadn't started off with LastPass, I would probably embrace **Dashlane** for my password management, though the premium pricing is quite a bit higher. They both have attractive interfaces, seamless synchronization and easy ways to change multiple passwords at once. NerdHerder Debra Whalen likes that Dashlane "keeps all of my personal info in one safe place with easy access." Dashlane gets bonus points for letting you choose whether you store your passwords locally or in the cloud.

DataVault Password Manager

A NerdHerder Favorite Password Tool

ascendo.co

NerdHerder Jeff Horn endorses **DataVault Password Manager** from Ascendo. "DataVault syncs between all my Apple devices (iPhone, iPad, iMac) so by changing one, they are all made up to date automatically. I use it dozens of times a day when in the office, on the road and at home." And in true nerd form, Jeff adds, "My DataVault password is in my will so that my family can find everything relevant in my life."

eWallet

Password Manager with Military-Grade Encryption

iliumsoft.com

Got a BlackBerry? **eWallet** has you covered. This multi-platform password manager is Kathy Dunn's favorite. "I can easily access all of my passwords in one place, which saves me time."

Also Check Out...

Have I Been Pwned?

Search Engine for Hacked Emails and Usernames
haveibeenpwned.com

If you're worried about your passwords, visiting **Have I Been Pwned?** can help you rest easier (or get really nervous). Enter your emails and usernames into the search engine, and the site scans millions of records that have been released after data breaches. A couple of my emails and one of my usernames have shown up on the lists, along with the data breach information with the sites and the dates.

SECURITY

Hot Topic:
Four Non-Tech Password
Management Techniques

If using a password manager makes you nervous, and you have used up all the sticky room space around your monitor, give these techniques a try.

1. Make Up a Phrase

Come up with a fun, memorable phrase for each site. For Netflix, you might choose, "I binge-watched the first eight Star Wars movies on Christmas Day 2015 (#truestory)!" Then you'd take that phrase and use the first letter from each word. So your password might be *Ib-wtf8SWmoCD2015(#ts)!*. (Feel free to use that one if you like.) The problem is that you'll still need to have a unique password for every site, so this may make your brain explode.

2. Sandwich the Site

This method is easier: Bury the name of the site in a familiar phrase. For example, you might choose, "I_love_Nerds_2017" as your phrase. Then your LinkedIn password might be *I_love_LinkedIn_Nerds_2017* and Facebook would be *I_love_Facebook_Nerds_2017*.

3. Carry a Card

The next step up from sticky notes is an innovative little site called **PasswordCard** (passwordcard.org). You generate a unique and complicated wallet-sized card that helps you choose random passwords for all your sites. PasswordCard also has an app so you can carry your card with you electronically.

4. Roll the Dice

Several attendees in my sessions have suggested a system called **Diceware** (world.std.com/~reinhold/diceware.html) to pick passwords. For each password, you will roll standard six-sided dice in accordance with very specific rules. Eventually you'll end up with random passwords with random words in a random order. Your Netflix password could be *amaze kombu bout ghana bogy*. You must memorize the password (from the site, "After you memorize your passphrase, burn your notes, pulverize the ashes and flush them down the toilet."). It's great for the occasional super-duper password, but don't forget that you must have a unique password for every single site you visit.

Browse More Efficiently

Every time a browser updates the software, you'll see faster loading, more security features and increased privacy. But you can also take more proactive steps to make your browsing more efficient and safe.

Start with...

Adblock Plus

Browser Adblocker that Prevents Pop-Ups, Tracking, Malware and More
adblockplus.org

Just by installing a quick plugin for your browser, you can speed up web pages and stop annoying ads from cluttering up your screen. I'm amazed at how fast pages load without the ads. You can find plenty of adblock options, but **Adblock Plus** is a favorite as an open-source product that works on a whole bunch of different browsers, including mobile ones.

Then Try...

Print Friendly

Multi-Platform Print Management Tool
printfriendly.com

Printliminator

Simple Bookmark for Print-Friendly Sites
nerdybff.com/printliminatorbookmark

Have you ever tried to print a simple 500-word article from the web only to end up with 14 pages of ads, promos and other webpage crapola? Both **Print Friendly** and **Printliminator** analyze websites and pages before you print, allowing you to eliminate graphics, ads, footers and other extraneous material that eats up ink and paper.

P.S.—NerdHerder Lisa Priepot loves Printliminator. "It makes web-sites print better, and you save tons of ink!"

Also Check Out...

Fast.com
Netflix Internet Speed Checker
fast.com

SpeedTest
Another Internet Speed Checker
speedtest.net

Most of us depend on a strong internet connection to make sure we can upload, download and access what we need from the web and the cloud. **Fast.com** and **SpeedTest** both run tests on your connection to make sure you're fast enough to do what you need to do. I've used them to prove to my provider that my connection wasn't as fast as it should be. And when I travel, I check a connection before choosing between my personal hotspot or the hotel's.

Down for Everyone or Just Me?
Utility to Discover Whether a Site is, Umm,
  Down for Everyone or Just You
downforeveryoneorjustme.com

Have you ever been surfing the web and come across a down page? Maybe I'm a little paranoid, but my first thought is always, "I wonder if this is down for everyone or just me?"

Guess what? There's a site for that. Just type the URL in question into the perfectly named site **downforeveryoneorjustme.com**. The service checks the offending site to see if it's an isolated problem.

PaperKarma

Junk Mail Eliminator

paperkarma.com

PaperKarma lets you snap a picture of the junk mail you receive, and they'll contact the company to remove you from the mailing list. Not only does it cut down on the junk mail that hides your kitchen table… it also helps companies save money on catalogs that you'll never open.

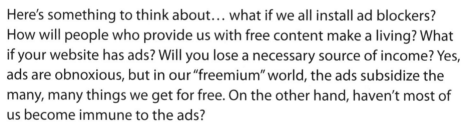

Hot Topic:
Are Adblockers Fair?

Here's something to think about… what if we all install ad blockers? How will people who provide us with free content make a living? What if your website has ads? Will you lose a necessary source of income? Yes, ads are obnoxious, but in our "freemium" world, the ads subsidize the many, many things we get for free. On the other hand, haven't most of us become immune to the ads?

One bright spot for advertisers who use pay-per-click advertising: your ads will still appear inside mobile apps, which is where most of the advertising clicks come from anyway these days.

Manage Spam: Email Edition

Any email you don't want is spam, from sincere offers from Nigerian princes to the newsletter you signed up for 3 years ago with gluten-free recipes. Thanks to these tech tools, you don't have to put up with spam in your inbox anymore.

Start with...

Unroll.me
Email Subscription Manager and Unsubscribe Tool
unroll.me

If your Gmail (Page 64) inbox (or Yahoo! or AOL or more) overflows with subscriptions, promotions and just plain old junk, **Unroll.me** can help (but first check out an important conversation we need to have about privacy issues, Page 30). It analyzes and categorizes your email, making it easy to unsubscribe from what you don't want and organize the rest into a daily or weekly digest.

Note: Unroll.me works wonderfully for things like newsletter subscriptions and social media notifications, but it can go all kinds of wrong with forum notifications. Experiment a little with the different types of subscriptions in your inbox to make it work for you.

Then Try...

Gmail

The Most Versatile Cloud-Based Email Service
gmail.com

Go to Page 64 for the full description of **Gmail**, but the tool belongs in this list because it's hands down the very best filter for removing spam from your inbox. Seriously.

Also Check Out...

To avoid getting on spammers' lists in the first place, create tempo-rary email addresses from **EmailOnDeck** (Page 123). When a site asks you to register to, for example, download a free resource, EmailOnDeck can provide an email that lasts just a few minutes. Keep the site open if you need to receive a confirmation email because your temporary email page is also a temporary inbox.

SECURITY

Manage Spam: Phone Edition

Have you noticed the increase in robocalls and missed number hang-ups from mystery numbers? Here are a handful of tools that will help you eliminate obnoxious calls.

Start with...

Truecaller

Mystery Number Identifier for Mobile Devices
truecaller.com

Truecaller compares mystery numbers with a crowdsourced list of known spammers. When you get a call from a number you don't recognize, you can search it on Truecaller to find out if others have reported it as spam. Some incoming calls will immediately show up as spammers without the extra step of cutting and pasting.

Check your tech: Some Android phones may build in this feature, and Apple is rumored to have something in the works.

Then Try...

Nomorobo

Registry to Remove Your Number from Robocall Lists
nomorobo.com

Register your phone numbers with **Nomorobo** to remove your VoIP landline from robocall lists, or pay a small monthly fee to register your mobile device number.

Also Check Out...

Mr Number

Another Call Block Tool
mrnumber.com

My attendees prefer **Mr Number** to block spam calls and texts. And I love the name better than Truecaller.

Travel

· ·

I want to . . .

TRAVEL

Organize Travel Plans

• •

Traveling in the age of the smartphone is more complicated than ever. Because we're tethered to both home and office via email, text and social media, we're expected to be able to respond in an airport just as quickly as if we were sitting on our couch.

Luckily technology can help us keep our travel plans organized so we can multitask on the go, no matter how far we're going.

Start with...

TripIt
Effortless Travel Organizer
tripit.com

TripCase
In Case You Hate TripIt
tripcase.com

The first time you use **TripIt**, you'll wonder how you ever lived without it. The concept is simple—just forward all your travel confirmations to plans@tripit.com, which is connected to the email address you use to forward. TripIt absorbs your confirmation and makes all the plans available on your mobile device. Besides the effortless transfer of travel details, TripIt links parts of your trip together, combining your flight, car rental and hotel under one trip. The modestly priced Pro version adds features such as real-time flight alerts plus fare watches. I've received more in fare refunds than I've spent on the yearly membership.

TripCase does just about the same things as TripIt—and it's free. The only paid option is the ability to track expenses by snapping pictures of receipts—just $5.99 a year.

NerdHerd members submitted more than 100 of their favorite tools for this book, and TripIt received the most thumbs up! Check out what your fellow nerds had to say.

Fran Rickenbach	When I'm planning multiple trips at a time, TripIt keeps all my reservations organized. It notifies me of gate arrival and departures, layover time and keeps my confirmation numbers so handy. Since I started using this I have never had to frantically search for flight or hotel Info.
John Silwonuk	TripIt keeps me organized.
Emily Arrowsmith	I love having all my trip details in one place at my fingertips!
Julie Perrine	TripIt coordinates ALL of your travel plans in one convenient place including maps, directions, destination highlights, and so much more! You can add details manually or simply forward your travel details by email to TripIt… and it organizes everything by trip in one convenient app tool including a printable itinerary.
Juan L. Martinez	I travel a lot, and TripIt is very helpful.
Raven Catlin	I love how it organizes my travel.

TRAVEL

Then Try...

HelloGbye
Textable Travel Agent Bot
hellogbye.com

Pana
Travel Agent Bot with Human Backup
pana.com

In the new world order, we're able to do more and more by texting back and forth with really smart computers. **HelloGbye** and **Pana** are subscription-based travel assistants that you can text to make travel plans. Message these tools with a travel request such as, "I need to fly to Denver on the 14th," and the bots will do the research for you and come back with options. Both allow you to coordinate plans with fellow travelers, and you have options to get help when travel plans go awry.

Also Check Out...

Google Trips   #CreepyButHelpful
Travel Organization for the Adventurous Tourist
google.com/trips

When you throw the family in the car for the best summer road trip ever, **Google Trips** is the perfect travel organizer. Google Trips grabs all the travel confirmations from your Gmail (Page 64) account and organizes them into a TripIt-style itinerary. Then the fun begins. The app helps you plan your trip, revealing sights and events along your way, ensuring you'll never miss the World's Largest Holstein Cow (the Salem Sue statue in New Salem, North Dakota, stands 38 feet tall) or the best fish and chips in the UK (Simpsons Fish and Chips, Cheltenham, won the 2016 Award).

NerdHerd Thumbs Up: Bonus Travel Tools

Our NerdHerders have even more travel tools to share.

Lola
Personal Travel Service for
   Hotels, Flights and More
lolatravel.com

App in the Air
Travel Organizer and Mileage Tracker
appintheair.mobi

Carolyn Rauch has some great insight about how she uses some advanced travel tools.

> *Pana is good, but **Lola** is absolutely incredibly amazing for booking hotel rooms. And it's free! I've had them spend days looking for the right hotels for me, and my reservation have always been solid. Also, I prefer **App in the Air** to Pana—the notifications and other features work better. Maybe just because it's older than Pana. And also App in the Air has this cool feature that shows how many miles you travel each year, and maps it! You can watch "yourself" go all around the country.*

Kayak
Airline Fare Search Tool
kayak.com

Alberta Hultman wants you guys to know about **Kayak**, a tool that searches all airlines for the lowest fare. "Kayak gets me started on seeing what to anticipate and who to book with."

Southwest App
Southwest Airline's Mobile App
southwest.com/mobile

Most (all?) major airlines have mobile apps that help you track your reservations, access your boarding passes and sometimes even book travel. NerdHerder Ronni Maestas likes **Southwest's** app for its ability to manage Southwest trips as well as partner airlines.

Track Mileage

If you're still logging miles into a little notebook in your dashboard, these apps are for you.

Start with...

Everlance
Mileage Tracking App with Expense Tracking
everlance.com

MileIQ
Mileage Tracking App
mileiq.com

The little errands you run all day add up: office supply runs for the office, volunteer carpool to the community fundraiser, back-and-forth trips to the doctor's office. And all those errands could be deductible, if only you would track them.

Everlance and **MileIQ** take the work out of tracking mileage. Both log your trips passively without you having to remember to open the app or start a tracker. At your convenience you can quickly classify your trips and get reports on your deductible miles, along with the current IRS rates. The info is ready to plop into your taxes for your well-earned credit.

Everlance goes a little further than MileIQ by letting you track other expenses as well as you travel down the road. Both tools will cost you about $60 a year. MileIQ is a NerdHerd favorite. Joyce Nakamura says, "It's automatic. I don't have to remember to turn it on. It detects the drive and calculates my route. All I have to do is categorize the drive—simple." And Missy Malechek adds, "MileIQ makes keeping up with your mileage happen in spite of you! My employer loves the report it produces… and I no longer have trips I am not reimbursed for because I forgot to write down my mileage. Pretty cool!"

Also Check Out...

ParkingPanda
Pre-Purchase Parking Service
parkingpanda.com

Nothing can spoil a day at the beach more than having to drive around forever looking for parking. **ParkingPanda** lets you find and reserve parking so you'll have the perfect spot without having to rely on luck. You can use the app to find spots on the go or plan ahead online. You can even find the occasional discount coupon.

TRAVEL

Discover New Sights and Sites

In 1996 my sister and I spent 6 months working our way around the country. Armed with a Rand McNally Road Atlas and a *Let's Go USA* travel guide, we visited 26 states without strangling each other.

We mapped our route with a highlighter and just crossed our fingers that we'd run across cool things to see. Now it's soooo much easier to plan the road trip of a lifetime (or even a Sunday drive).

Start with...

Roadtrippers
Road Trip Planner
roadtrippers.com

Roadtrippers lets you make your plan to get from A to B, whether you want the most direct route to save money or the drive that brings you past the best taco stands in Southern California. You can use the app or the site to plot start and end points, then have fun with all the possibilities in between. Share your trips with friends to make sure everyone sees what she wants to see.

A side note about Roadtrippers... it's addictive. I stopped by the site to check it out for this book, and before I knew it, I was planning a vacation and a drive from San Diego to Portland. Poof! Two hours disappeared.

Then Try...

Detour
Location-Based Audio Walking Tours
detour.com

The only bad thing about the **Detour** audio walking tour app is that it's not available in every city. The location-based tours will entertain and educate you as you explore new locations as well as cities you've known all your life. Hear filmmaker Ken Burns tell you the story of the Brooklyn Bridge as you walk across. Or listen to the story of what may be America's first serial killer as you discover Austin with the help of the Radiolab podcasters. You can also synchronize your tour with friends to wander together. The tours are totally worth their $5 price.

HISTORY Here
App to Discover an Area's History
history.com/history-here

I live less than 2 miles from the first Franciscan mission in what was once known as The Californians, a province of New Spain. **HISTORY Here** helped me discover the mission as well as other historical sites in my area. This app by the HISTORY Channel will delight history buffs who love to discover fun facts about the places they visit.

Also Check Out...

Yelp Monacle
Location-Based Business Finder with Reviews
yelp.com

I bet you've heard of Yelp, the review-based business directory that lets you discover

#NerdPartyTrick

restaurants, services and more near you. But you might not know about the **Yelp Monocle** tool, which is hidden in the "more" section of the app. The feature uses your camera's viewfinder to let you look through the lens. Then you'll see the reviews of the restaurants in your line of sight hovering above the buildings. It's another great party trick.

Heads Up
Ellen DeGeneres' Award-Winning Family Game
ellentv.com/page/2013/04/23/heads-up

How can you entertain the kids on a long road trip (if they look up from their phones)? Break out **Heads Up**! You hold your phone on your forehead, and the app displays a word or phrase that you have to guess with clues from other players. She has a version for kids and several other fun games. NerdHerder Joanne St-Pierre suggested it simply because "it is so fun to play!"

Hot Topic:
Is There Really an App
for Everything?

Yep. These bathroom-related apps are proof.

RunPee
Database App that Shares the Best Time for
   a Bathroom Run During a Movie
runpee.com

When you're drinking super-triple sodas while watching the summer's best blockbusters in a movie theater, you might need to take a break. **RunPee** tells you the best time to run to the restroom so you don't miss anything critical.

SitOrSquat
Bathroom Review App Brought to You by Charmin
sitorsquat.com

Yep. It is what you think it is. **SitOrSquat** helps you find clean public restrooms. The app hasn't been updated in a while, but people are still reviewing bathrooms regularly. One annoying thing: The fine print you have to read before being able to leave a review is ridiculous. And you must put your birthdate in just to visit the site. Huh?

Stay Safe on the Go

Have you ever seen Creepy Stalker Guy hanging out near your car in a dark parking lot? Or felt uncomfortable answering a knock at the door in a hotel? Or walked home after dark alone? These apps link you to technology that links you to a support system that can help you feel safer.

Start with...

SafeTrek

Safety Button that Reaches Authorities in a Flash
safetrekapp.com

SafeTrek was developed by college students for college students. If you're worried about your safety, you open the app with one tap then hold your thumb on the big button and just keep walking. When you take your thumb off the button, you have 10 seconds to put in a code. If the code is not entered, the system is notified, and SafeTrek sends your location, name and number to the nearest police station.

I guess we'll have to trust that it works because I'm scared to do a test run and end up with a hotel room full of policemen. I am happy just paying my $30 a year for peace of mind.

Then Try...

Companion

Safety App for a Network of Friends
companionapp.io

If you've ever had to text someone to tell him you're safe at home, **Companion** app might make it easier. Just designate your friends and family as companions, and they can keep an eye on you as you travel to your destination. Then with a tap you can let them know you're safe. This free app also has a Smart Trigger that raises an alarm to alert your companions that you might need help. *Note: If you don't have any friends, use SafeTrek.*

EmergenSee

Emergency App with Live Video Streaming

emergensee.com

EmergenSee has the best characteristics of both SafeTrek and Companion. You can create a network of friends who will keep an eye on you, or pay about $9 a month for professional monitoring that connects you to emergency personnel. The cool addition is that the app includes live video streaming so you could show a contact what's happening in real time and keep a record of a challenging situation.

Also Check Out...

Nextdoor

Social Network for Neighborhoods

nextdoor.com

As Sesame Street folks used to ask, "Who are the people in your neighborhood?" **Nextdoor** is a social network that keeps you abreast of what's happening where you live. You can find local recommendations for plumbers, reliable babysitters, garage sale hotspots—and, more importantly—news about suspicious characters and neighborhood crime.

Last Message

Android App that Alerts Friends of a Low Battery

fat-brain.it

NerdHerd member Michelle Grachek looks to **Last Message** to text, email, Facebook message or tweet the individuals you select to alert them when your phone is about to die. "I am constantly at the end of my battery life with my phone. It helps for someone to know that I am unavailable in case of an emergency."

Navigate Smartly

· ·

In the old days, driving to a new place involved a Rand McNally Road Atlas and the ability to refold a map. Now we're all accustomed to electronic navigation systems that guide us through every turn and help us avoid traffic and discover new sights.

Start with...

Google Maps

Worldwide Navigation System with Real-Time Updates
google.com/maps

Waze

Crowdsourced Navigation App with
   Real-Time Updates
waze.com

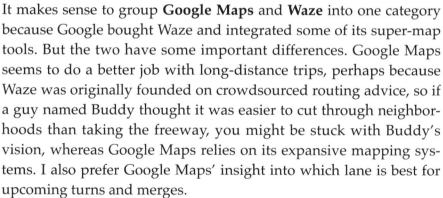

It makes sense to group **Google Maps** and **Waze** into one category because Google bought Waze and integrated some of its super-map tools. But the two have some important differences. Google Maps seems to do a better job with long-distance trips, perhaps because Waze was originally founded on crowdsourced routing advice, so if a guy named Buddy thought it was easier to cut through neighborhoods than taking the freeway, you might be stuck with Buddy's vision, whereas Google Maps relies on its expansive mapping systems. I also prefer Google Maps' insight into which lane is best for upcoming turns and merges.

But Waze has personality and friends, and that may trump better navigation for in-town travel. Both apps have real-time traffic updates and advice, but Waze's info comes from other users on the road, alerting you of slowdowns, hazards and cops. You can connect with fellow drivers and send neighborly honks to your friends. You can also change the navigation voice in Waze to pop culture icons such as Star Wars' C-3PO, who will help you nerd out on your commute with messages about the next turn. Plus, and perhaps most importantly, you can send your route and ETA to people waiting on you to avoid those "Where are you now?" calls.

Waze was second only to TripIt (Page 138) for the most praise by the NerdHerd.

Jamie Rice	Waze gets me to where I need to be, sends alerts when I need to leave, provides route options, alerts me to traffic and hazards—and more!
Ellie Taylor	Waze saved me time with accident alerts on so many occasions.
Loretta Peskin	It's better than my Toyota navigation system.
Vikki Mitchell	Waze gives directions on the app as well as being inner active and having traffic reports.
Lydia Rouzeau	It keeps you informed of traffic conditions including what may be coming up on the road and police lookout to reduce speed!

Then Try...

HERE WeGo

International Map App with Transit Options
here.com

HERE shares many of the characteristics of Google Maps, including the capability to download maps and use them offline to avoid big data bills when you're traveling overseas. It has maps for hundreds of major cities around the world, plus 3D maps of thousands of malls, airports and other facilities.

CityMaps2Go

International City Map App with Travel Insight
ulmon.com

CityMaps2Go is a great app for your backpacking trip through Europe. It's a favorite for its colorful, easy-to-read city guides and bonus cultural facts and articles.

Also Check Out...

FlightAware

Flight Tracker with Airport Delay Info
flightaware.com

As NerdHerder Laura Young says, "Do you ever look up in the sky and wonder, 'Where is that plane going?' or 'Where did that plane come from?' Do you ever wonder where your plane was before your flight or if your friend's flight will be on time? **FlightAware** has the answers."

The app tells you what's above you, plus gives you updates on flights, latest information on airport delays and other crucial travel info.

Amaze your friends: Ask Siri to tell   **#NerdPartyTrick**
you what planes are overhead.

Hot Topic:
What Are Some Travel Tools
for Special Travel Needs?

Some travel apps offer a helping hand for special challenges on the road.

brettapproved
Site that Helps People with Disabilities Travel Easier
brettapproved.com

If you're wondering whether a "wheelchair accessible" hotel has a truly navigable ramp, check out the ratings on **brettapproved**. Unsurprisingly founded by a guy named Brett, the site lets disabled travelers discover and rate places to eat, stay and play.

BringFido
Site to Discover Pet-Friendly Businesses
bringfido.com

If you just can't leave your pet pig at home, search **BringFido** for pet-friendly restaurants, hotels, parks and more.

Travefy
Group Travel Management
travefy.com

Coordinating travel for family reunions, best friend road trips and staff retreats can be a royal pain. **Travefy** lets you share itineraries, travel ideas and other logistics to bring everyone together in the right place at the right time.

Search for Travel Bargains

On your next flight, you could sit next to someone who is paying hundreds of dollars less than you to go to the same place. These tools even the playing field when it comes to finding the best prices for travel.

Start with...

Hopper
Travel Shopping App to Find the Best Time to Fly
hopper.com

This travel app caused me all kinds of hassle... not because it's not helpful but because it is TOO helpful! **Hopper** lets you plug in details for a trip you want to take, and it will make predictions about the price and tell you when it's best to buy. You'll find yourself shopping for flights for January, and all of a sudden you'll be putting in alerts for the best prices to visit all your Facebook friends.

Then Try...

Google Flights
Google's Travel Tool with Price Alerts
google.com/flights

This is yet another step in Google's plan to take over our lives. **Google Flights** lets you search for flights on most major airlines to compare fares, schedules, stops and more. Search results show you cost-saving tips like "Save $32 if you leave the day before and depart the day after." Google also gives you the option to track the trip to receive price alerts.

Hipmunk

Travel Shopping App with Adorable Mascot

hipmunk.com

With **Hipmunk** you can quickly sort travel options by departure or arrival time, and it has an "agony" filter that reveals the flights with the best routes and fewest hassles. It doesn't really save you money, but I do love that little mascot.

Also Check Out...

GasBuddy

Tool that Tracks Gas Prices to Find the Lowest Near You

gasbuddy.com

This really works! **GasBuddy** searches prices of all the gas stations within driving distance to help you find the best rates.

Delegate

● ●

I want to . . .

DELEGATE

Automate Tasks

Without even realizing it, you probably do the same tasks over and over, such as checking the weather, saving attachments from emails, tweeting your latest blog post on Twitter.

Though it takes just a few minutes to complete each task, these little jobs add up fast, and you probably have better uses of your time in today's crazy-busy lifestyle.

Start with...

IFTTT
Free Multi-App Automator
ifttt.com

IFTTT, which stands for "if this then that," is one of a category of tools that will help you automate some of these little tasks so you don't have to think about them. Just connect your cloud-based services, social media accounts, phones and more, and create little recipes (called "applets") that trigger under your rules. In May of 2017, IFTTT took the applets to a new level by letting the IFTTT community create multi-step recipes that automate things even more.

For example, you can set a rule to send you an email at 7 AM if it's going to rain that day. Or a rule that saves any photos you share on Facebook into your Dropbox folder. Or a rule that blinks your lights off and on with team colors when your football team makes a touchdown.

IFTTT works with a number of devices and gadgets, venturing into the world we know as "The Internet of Things." You can automate tasks with Nest thermostats, Philips Hue light bulbs and many fitness trackers. IFTTT's apps also create opportunities to use specific iOS and Android features, such as location tracking and selfies.

You can browse through the thousands   #NerdPartyTrick
of applets that other IFTTT users have
shared or use the wizard to walk through setting up your own. My
favorite party trick: Set up an IFTTT applet to ring your phone with
a touch of a button to get you out of a boring meeting.

Then Try...

Microsoft Flow
Microsoft's Multi-App Automator
flow.microsoft.com

Microsoft Flow is an IFTTT-like tool built into its suite of products.
Log in to your Microsoft account on the website and choose the flows
(recipes) you want to happen automatically, such as sending an
approval email when a new item is added in SharePoint.

Zapier
Free/Paid Multi-App Automator
zapier.com

IFTTT is free, but it doesn't connect with everything. **Zapier** has many
more connected apps in its stable, but some of them require a paid
account.

Also Check Out...

Tasker
Android Device Automator
In Google Play Store

Workflow
Apple Device Automator
workflow.is

Tasker and **Workflow** are automators that make your mobile devices
more efficient. You can set up little automations to run for common

DELEGATE

phone tasks, such as reading the news (have Siri read it to you), posting to Facebook, combining photos into a GIF, letting meeting attendees know you're running late, and much, much more.

Tasker fans have become a little cranky in the reviews lately, with a common complaint about how complicated it can be to set up a task. Workflow has glowing praise and lots of pre-set templates.

Pushbullet
Notification and Sharing Center for Texts, Files and More
pushbullet.com

Have you ever had to go through all kinds of strange iterations to get something from your phone to your computer? **Pushbullet** links multiple devices and services so you can minimize the number of places you have to go to perform common tasks. You can hook up your favorite messaging apps so you can text from your computer, or instantly share a picture from your phone with your computer and other devices.

NerdHerd Thumbs Up:
Schedule Social Media Posts

Buffer
Social Media Scheduler
buffer.com

NerdHerder Kathy Wilson manages social media for her organization, and she uses **Buffer** to help. Buffer schedules, tracks, and reports on social media posts. "It schedules all of my social media posts in a very easy, straightforward way. The app has lots of flexibility, even with the free version, and provides great stats."

Hot Topic:
Virtual Assistants

In the last couple of years, voice-activated services like Apple's Siri and Google's voice tool have evolved from being a quick way to launch an app to being an all-knowing, all-understanding "virtual assistant." These services and devices can now integrate with many areas of our world, such as our cloud services (like Dropbox, Page 14) and social media. Now instead of having to search online for a product or grab our phone to hail a car, we can just ask Amazon's always-on Alexa to handle the tasks.

These assistants are improving every day with the help of more cloud-connected services and automated helpers such as IFTTT and Zapier.

DELEGATE

Outsource Work Tasks

One of the best things I've done for my business is to recognize that I can't do it all. I regularly outsource tasks and projects rather than trying to do them myself. It's not as expensive as you might think with these services.

Start with...

Fancy Hands

U.S.-Based Virtual Assistants for Small Tasks

fancyhands.com

If there's one tool a busy professional needs, it's an extra set of hands. **Fancy Hands** employs a stable of U.S.-based virtual assistants who take annoying little tasks off your list so you can concentrate on getting work done. Fancy Hands helps me set appointments, track down lost mail, transcribe business cards, create cool graphics, research tech tools—you name it—all kinds of little 20-minute tasks that can take me out of work mode and make me lose more time.

Fancy Hands is FAST! I've submitted tasks on weekends and holidays, and almost all of them are completed and back to me within the hour. It doesn't promise to make any type of deadline, but you can indicate that a task is time-sensitive when you send it in.

Prices start at $30 a month for up to five tasks.

Then Try...

Fiverr

Freelance Marketplace for Small Jobs
   Starting at Five Bucks

fiverr.com

Need to build a new website? Or create a fancy intro video that makes your logo dance? Or revamp your marketing material? Help is on the way!

When I need something done, my first thought is always **Fiverr**. Fiverr is a marketplace of literally thousands of people who do all kinds of stuff—starting at five bucks (a fiver, get it?). The site presents the engagements in an attractive format and gives you plenty of ways to search for the right freelancer. If you can't find a gig you want, you can write a description of your project and request bids.

It's smart to choose three to five designers for the same project to see which one gives you a better product. You're still not out very much money, and you'll get a variety of results that you can build on.

Fiverr gigs will often cost you more than five bucks because of the add-ons. You may pay extra for a rush job or for the addition of color or a background to a graphic. You're still paying very little for someone's hard work, so the upgrades are easily worth it.

NerdHerder Frank Lessing also loves Fiverr. "You can get professionally done services at a low cost—many are really $5."

Upwork
Freelance Community for Larger Projects
upwork.com

Although Fiverr is awesome, you're not always going to get away with a $5 project to advance your business. For larger projects, you can find any number of freelancer marketplaces; and on each site, you can find thousands and thousands of proven experts who can help you with every imaginable task. I think of these types of sites as Craigslist on steroids where you can find potential contractors, evaluate their ratings, keep track of their work and control the payment.

When I need to outsource a large project, I head to **Upwork**. You describe your project and set the parameters: your budget, your timeline, your hopes and dreams for a successful project. Then you open your project for bids to the marketplace. To find the right person, you might want to search the providers and invite your favorites to bid. If you're commissioning an illustration, for example, hop around in their portfolios to find a designer with a style you like.

After you declare a winner on Upwork, the site serves as a super-efficient project management tool. You and your new contractor agree on the project terms. On larger projects, you can divide up payments with milestones. As you work, the system acts like your own Basecamp site (Page 39). Every email you send is cataloged in the system. Every file you exchange is kept in the workroom. Every milestone is tracked. The system even has communication tools for collaboration with your contractor.

Also Check Out...

TaskRabbit
Personal Task Service
taskrabbit.com

Amazon Home Services
Amazon's Personal Task Service
nerdybff.com/tryamazonhomeservices

Need to mount your flat-screen TV? Or maybe assemble a new foosball table? There's an app for that. A number of services keep handy people in your area on speed dial, making it easy for you to arrange for a plumber, painter, yard person or general fix-it guy. **TaskRabbit** was one of the early services. **Amazon Home Services** popped up in 2015. Like many of the services in the sharing economy, these companies let you read profiles, skills and recommendations of service providers before you hire them to come into your home.

Finance

· ·

I want to . . .

FINANCE

163

Track Receipts and Expenses

• •

OK, 'fess up. Do you have a pile of wrinkled, stained, faded receipts sitting around your office that you're supposed to do something with? It's time to take control with these receipt management tools.

Start with...

Shoeboxed

Expense Manager for Paper and Digital Receipts
shoeboxed.com

Shoeboxed is a service that lets you snap a picture of something you need transcribed, or, even better, lets you physically send stuff to someone else who will unwrinkle and decipher the hard-to-read contents to extract the important info.

It's been around for quite some time. About ten bucks a month will let you send in up to 50 documents a month, including things such as business cards, documents and receipts. It'll scan and categorize everything for you and provide you a beautiful portal where you can export the organized information for expense reports, taxes, contact management and more.

Then Try...

Expensify

Expense Manager with SmartScan
expensify.com

Expensify is my second favorite expense tracking tool. You can snap pictures of your receipts on the go, just like Shoeboxed, but Expensify goes further in giving you a full financial picture by integrating credit card and bank statements.

A skill they call SmartScan helps Expensify technology automatically categorize your scans. Expensify also gives you all kinds of ways of managing your receipts, including synchronizing through QuickBooks and SaneBox (Page 66).

Kimberly Lilley is a Legacy NerdHerder as well as an Expensify fan. "I used to be TERRIBLE about submitting my expense reports for work… it came up on EVERY review. Once we got Expensify, that all changed."

Wally
Easy Expense Tracker
wally.me

My NerdHerd friend Mary C. Kelly, Ph.D., is a brilliant economist (like listed on "best of" lists for economists). She loves **Wally** to track her expenses because she says it's easier than other systems. A thumbs up from her means something.

Also Check Out...

FileThis
Financial Statement Fetching Tool
filethis.com

I don't know about your early spring, but things can get a little prickly around our house when my husband does our taxes. One of the sticking points used to be the gathering of all the statements. He was always waiting on me to get my credit card and bank paperwork into his hands.

FileThis has eased the tension. The service automatically fetches your bank statements, credit card paperwork and more. I set up a Dropbox folder for all the PDFs, and my husband just opens the folder during tax time and grabs what he needs without bugging me. Heaven.

Manage Budgets and Spending

• •

I probably shouldn't be the one to tell you about budgeting tools because I'm absolutely the worst at keeping track of my spending. But if I did aim to balance my checkbook every month, boy howdy, I'd use these tools.

Start with...

Mint
Award-Winning Budget Management Tool
mint.com

Mint, I tell you, Mint, Mint, Mint. This personal finance budget and money manager is always at the top of any list of best money tools. If you're new to money management tools, start here. Just ask everybody.

You Need a Budget
Low-Priced(ish) Budget Management Tool
youneedabudget.com

You guys know how much I love free stuff, so it's a little painful to recommend something that's $50 a year. People adore **YNAB** (that's what the cool kids call it) for personal budgeting, although there's much discussion about whether it can replace your business book-keeping. BONUS: Students get YNAB for free for a year!

Then Try...

Credit Karma
Credit-Checking Tool
creditkarma.com

We all should be incredibly paranoid about credit monitoring sites. Many of them require a credit card for "free monitoring," and then the site charges your card every month even though you stopped monitoring your numbers, like a gym membership you never use. It took me a while to believe that **Credit Karma** was really not going to start draining my credit card with monthly charges once I signed up. But it kept its word, and I now keep track of my actual credit score with no strings attached. Yay for Credit Karma, and it is incredibly convenient and easy for me.

Also Check Out...

Digit
Delightful Text-Based Savings Chatbot
digit.co

Penny
Text-Based Budget Chatbot with an Attitude
pennyapp.io

These tools are so much fun! Both **Digit** and **Penny** are chatbots that work through text messaging. Penny presents itself as an adorable girl named, well, Penny, who tracks your expenses, helps you save and keeps you in the know.

I used Digit for about 6 months, loving the quirky GIFs and comments it would send as the system snuck small amounts out of checking and into savings based on my spending patterns. I was able to squirrel away several hundred dollars without feeling a strain. I also like the "Goalmoji" feature, which lets you choose an emoji as a goal, such as 👠 for that new pair of Converse hi-tops. In 2017 they introduced a subscription model for the service but bumped up the bonus you receive if you let your money sit in their account for a little while.

Save Money

. . . .

It's easier than you think to discover sales and rebates with the help of technology. Here are some of my readers' favorite apps for discounts.

Start with...

Ibotta
Cash-Back App for Rebates and Sales
ibotta.com

People who love couponing are passionate about **Ibotta**. Just download the app and search for rebates that unlock cash rewards. To get a rebate offer, you need to complete a small task, such as watching a sponsor video or sharing a post on Facebook. Then you can redeem your reward in person from one of dozens of participating stores, and Ibotta puts cash into your PayPal account.

You used to have to snap a picture of a receipt to get your rebate, but now many stores have instant scan tools (like Walmart's QR code) that will upload your receipt without the added step.

RetailMeNot
Coupon Site with Mobile App for Bargains
retailmenot.com

One of the best ways to save money while shopping online is to use promotion codes at checkout. While there are several sites to use, **RetailMeNot** is easy to use and has a variety of retailers. Some retailers do not allow posting of codes by users; in this case, check the comments to see if there is anything useful. Also check the maximum number of codes you can use per order because some sites let you use more than one.

Bonus! The RetailMeNot app uses geolocation capabilities to let you know when the store you're near has coupons and sales.

Then Try...

Honey

Browser Extension for Coupon Codes and Savings
joinhoney.com

Although I'm partial to RetailMeNot, **Honey** may be more convenient for finding deals at online stores. The tool is integrated into your browser and alerts you when the site has a promotion code. And if you're an Amazon addict like I am, Honey works extra hard to find you the best prices from Amazon sellers that Amazon may not show you. And if that wasn't enough, Honey may share any commission it makes from your shopping by giving you cash back on your purchase.

Key Ring

Loyalty Card Organizer
keyringapp.com

If you're like me, chances are you have a pile of grocery, pharmacy and other loyalty cards in your wallet, and a couple of peeling, pathetic ones on your key ring. These are the cards you need to scan to receive store discounts and garner loyalty points.

Key Ring is a handy smartphone app that allows you to enter all your loyalty programs into your phone so you don't have to carry the physical cards anymore. To enter your cards, just snap a picture of the card's barcode, and your card is permanently and instantly cataloged in your app.

In addition, the loyalty programs frequently offer other discounts and specials through the app and makes it easier for you to sign up for new cards as well. NerdHerder Jason Burton says, "I love this app because I don't need to keep 20 different rewards cards in my wallet. I just pull up the app and let the store scan the barcode!"

FINANCE

Also Check Out...

Ebates

Rebate Tool for Online Purchases

ebates.com

NerdHerder Di Richards gives a shout out to **Ebates**, a site that lets you shop many stores online through its portal, then rewards you with coupons and cash back. Di is thrilled. "It's helping me save money!"

StubHub

Event Ticket Marketplace

stubhub.com

Get the sniffles before the Patriots' game? You can sell your ticket on **StubHub** for any price you choose. NerdHerder Steven Jones loves to buy and sell tickets on the site. Although hot tickets can go for big bucks, more than half of the tickets are listed at face value or below.

Cut the Cable Cord (Hardware)

· ·

This section is for my father, who groans about cable bills but puts off cutting the cord. Maybe a little spotlight on his reticence will prompt him to take action (assuming he reads this... you there, Papa?).

With the combination of inexpensive hardware and a few monthly subscriptions to streaming video sites, you'll have more TV and movies than you'll ever be able to watch.

Start with...

Apple TV

Apple's Streaming Device
apple.com/tv

Apple TV is a streaming player that allows you to watch iTunes, streaming services, TV apps, YouTube and others from your television. Updates make it possible for Siri to search for programming and even control your home's lights and thermostat from the TV. Pricing starts at $149.

Roku

One of the Original Streaming Video Devices
roku.com

Roku is a streaming player that allows you to watch free channels, subscribe to streaming services (such as Netflix and Hulu) and rent TV shows and movies. Currently, there are five Roku players to choose from, ranging from $40 to $130. I bought one ages ago, and we find it more reliable than the apps linked to our smart TV.

Then Try...

Amazon Fire Stick
Amazon's Answer to Roku
amazon.com/firestick

Amazon Fire Stick is a portable stick that connects to your TV's HDMI port, giving you a range of television, apps, games... even news and sports networks. The newer devices use the voice recognition features of Alexa, Amazon's virtual assistant.

Chromecast
Google's Answer to Roku
google.com/chromecast

Chromecast is Google's streaming player. This gadget gives you the ability to play your favorite entertainment from your phone to your TV. The cost is $35.

Also Check Out...

HDTV Antenna
High-Tech Rabbit Ears for Your Modern TVs

If you long for the days when you scrunched tin foil onto the antenna on your TV to get local stations, you may enjoy this upgrade. One of the major benefits is the ability to get live news and sports without the cable bill. A quick search on Amazon for HDTV antennas will bring up a host of inexpensive devices that can pull over-the-air programming to your TV. For a couple hundred more, add a DVR like Tablo to record your favorite shows.

I bought a nice antenna for around $70. It picked up about 40 channels, including local broadcasts. More than half of them were Spanish-language channels. I speak French and a West African language called Bambara, so I was pretty much out of luck.

NerdHerd Thumbs Up: Unlimited Music

YouTube Music
Custom Music Mixes for Your Style
music.youtube.com

Is YouTube's streaming music subscription worth the price? Absolutely, says NerdHerder Heather Rae Osborne.

YouTube Music hosts endless hours of music at a low cost, and it learns what you like as you listen. It creates custom channels based on your likes and listening habits, artist stations, favorites, etc. It has far more song options than Pandora any day. You can watch it with video on or off and take it anywhere you go, as it works well on cellular and Wi-Fi (beach, work, car) and offline (for air travel).

FINANCE

Cut the Cable Cord (Services)
• •

People have crunched the numbers to see if cutting the cord really saves money after you replace all your cable services with streaming apps that charge subscription fees. But since many of us subscribe to some of these services on top of cable, I would bet that the overall price will decrease.

Here's a handy guide to some of the most popular streaming media services.

Amazon Prime Video	Streams popular movies, TV shows and original programming through Amazon devices, apps and the web.	Some first-run programs and hit movies are available to rent or buy, but many are included in an Amazon Prime membership. A live streaming membership is coming soon.
Hulu	Best for just-missed TV shows and more current programs.	Starts at $7.99 a month. A new live streaming option comes in at around $40 a month.
Netflix	Ah. A classic. Netflix started out as a service that mailed DVDs to those of us too lazy to go to Blockbuster (remember those?). Now Netflix is a major player in the online streaming market.	Starts at $7.99 a month.
Sling TV	Stream live shows and on-demand entertainment including lots of live sports.	Starts at $20 a month.

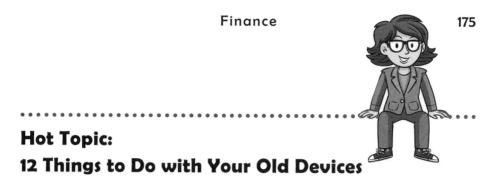

Hot Topic:
12 Things to Do with Your Old Devices

Many of us upgrade our phones every couple of years, which can lead to the dead-eye stare of an old smart device as it sits lonely in the junk drawer.

Here are a dozen ways you can repurpose your old device even after you move on to the shiny new gadget.

1. **Contribute to the Greater Good**
   BOINC
   Research Center that Uses the Power in
      Your Gadgets to Fight for Academic Research
   boinc.berkeley.edu

   Folding@Home
   Research Center that Focuses on Understanding Diseases
   folding.stanford.edu

   I'm starting off with my favorite idea first. Researchers have found a way to put the unused processing power of your devices to work on important research projects. The Berkeley Open Infrastructure for Network Computing, affectionately known as **BOINC** (giggle), links researchers with the power of a computing grid that taps into individual devices. You can hook up your old computer or Android device to work on climate studies, humanitarian research, astronomy projects and much more. Another service, **Folding@Home**, gives your computing power to researchers working on understanding diseases such as AIDS, Huntington's, Parkinson's and even cancer.

2. Keep Your Home Safe (Or Watch the Kitties from Work)

Alfred
Security Camera System that Works with Old Devices
alfred.camera

Manything
Security Camera System that Offers Online Storage
manything.com

Old devices are wonderful as security cameras. Both **Alfred** and **Manything** are free apps that let you set up devices as motion-sensing cameras around your house and monitor the video from afar. Manything also has optional cloud-based video storage starting at $2.99 a month.

3. Be Prepared for Emergencies

When you upgrade, wipe your old phone and insert a pre-paid SIM card. Then throw it into a junk drawer until you have a phone emergency. Bonus prep idea: buy a solar-powered device charger to bring the emergency phone to life if the power goes out.

4. Install a Dashcam

Nexar
Dashboard Camera App for Your Device
getnexar.com

Nexar combines your device's own sensory-gathering info (like speed, etc.) with traditional dashcam video monitoring to create a record of sudden stops, traffic events and more driving hazards.

5. Get to Where You're Going

Both Google Maps (Page 149) and HERE Maps (Page 151) let you download maps in advance, then navigate the world without data.

6. Create a Media Center

Purchase a video cable to connect your device to a monitor or TV, then load up your device with all your streaming media apps: Hulu, Netflix, Amazon Prime and more.

7. Keep an Eye on the Baby

Baby Monitor 3G

Baby Monitoring App that Uses Your Old Devices
babymonitor3g.com

Apps such as **Baby Monitor 3G** let you set up your old devices to listen for baby cries and general kid-watching activities.

8. Wake Up with Style

The charging station for my phone is in the living room, and when I need an alarm to get up for an early-morning flight, I stress about running out of juice. Set your old device up as an alarm (with the cool tools on Page 202) or even a sleep monitor to end the back-and-forth swapping of your primary device.

9. Create a Digital Photo Album

Share your online photo albums with friends and family (read: Grandparents!) to keep the most updated family photos playing on everyone's old devices. (P.S.—Want to send the grandparents real photo albums? Check out Page 231.)

10. Use Your Device as a Remote Control

SURE Universal Remote for TV
TV and Smart Device Remote for Android
tekoia.com/sure-universal

A quick search of the Google Play Store reveals dozens of apps like **SURE Universal Remote for TV** that enable you to turn your Android phone or tablet into a remote control for your TV and other Wi-Fi–connected devices. Apple limits using your device as a remote for, unsurprisingly, Apple products.

11. Donate to a Charity

Cell Phones for Soldiers
Donation Site for Old Devices
cellphonesforsoldiers.com

AmericanCellPhoneDrive.org
Charity Donation Site for Old Devices
americancellphonedrive.org

Cell Phones for Soldiers refurbishes old devices for, believe it or not, soldiers. Go to **AmericanCellPhoneDrive.org** to find local drives that support a number of causes.

12. Get Some Cash

Gazelle
Company that Buys Old Computers and Gadgets
gazelle.com

I've sold a couple of older computers to **Gazelle**. They make it easy to send in old devices to receive cash or Amazon gift cards. Using Gazelle you can also set up your own electronics drive for a charity group and get a 15% commission.

Personal Growth and Career

I want to . . .

GROWTH/CAREER

Create Resumes and CVs

• •

Not long ago LinkedIn killed one of my favorite hidden features: the ability to create an instant resume with a couple of clicks through its own resume tool. But a few tools still make it pretty easy to organize your info and design a great resume.

Start with...

Resumonk

Online Resume Builder with LinkedIn Import
resumonk.com

Not only do I like the name **Resumonk**, I also like the capabilities. The best part is that you can import the PDF of your LinkedIn profile to give you a great starting point for organizing the bits and pieces of your career. As with all these resume tools, you should expect to pay a modest amount for the upgrade to get all the features and remove any branding. But it's worth it to represent yourself well on job interviews.

Then Try...

Kickresume

Online Resume Creator with Personal Websites
kickresume.com

Kickresume also lets you upload a document with your existing resume, though it doesn't claim that they import the LinkedIn profile. But this tool stands out because you can also create a personal website that highlights your resume points, plus samples of your work and more facts that could get you hired.

Also Check Out...

ResumUP

Online Resume Creator with Infographic and Interactive Sites
resumup.com

I used a red font for headings the last time I applied for a job. Apparently, the flashiness earned me a place in the "nope" pile, until an assistant flipped through the rejects and took a liking to the color and put me back into the pile for consideration. That's as big of a risk as I've ever taken in job hunting.

I love playing with the resume tools on **ResumUP**, but I have no idea if a splashy, colorful timeline graphic would get me a job. ResumUP hooks up with your LinkedIn account to pull in your info, letting you choose to display the info in a standard resume or in interactive time-lines with lots of graphics and colors.

NerdHerd Thumbs Up:
Golf for Your Downtime

The Masters Tournament
Golf App
masters.com

Have a lot of extra time while you're job hunting? Fill your hours obsessing about golf! NerdHerder Tim Zielenbach says **The Masters Tournament** app is "all Masters, all the time." While golf isn't really my thing, Tim is a huge fan. "Golf's Holiest Week takes place in Augusta each April. This is a very thorough app that provides a ton of data, news and video as the event progresses, as well as a deep vault of video from the event's 80-year history."

GROWTH/CAREER

Launch a Blog or Website

· ·

Small business folks often seek professionals to build major projects like new websites or a blog. If you're a do-it-yourself nerd, give these blog builders a try.

Start with...

WordPress
Leading Site Builder for Blogs and Websites
wordpress.com

Starting a **WordPress** blog or website is easy, for both personal and business use. For a free hosted site with a URL such as nerdybest-friend.wordpress.com, simply create an account and pick a name at WordPress.com. There, you can also purchase various upgrades, including a custom URL if you want your blog or site to live at nerdybestfriend.com. If you want total control—including a custom URL, a wide variety of plug-ins and the capability to sell your own advertising—you can download the free WordPress software from WordPress.org; but you must arrange and pay for hosting of the site.

The next step in building your site with WordPress is choosing a theme, and here's where the magic begins. You can choose from thousands of free themes, or for less than $100, you can buy an easy-to-install framework for a full site, complete with the embedded blog for dynamic content, or not. I find great templates from Envato (Page 247) and **WooThemes** (woothemes.com). My assistant, Molly, loves **Elegant Themes** (elegantthemes.com). You can further personalize your site with any of the thousands of plug-ins and widgets to do everything from embed video to automatically tweet your posts to Twitter to install a carousel-type photo gallery.

Then Try...

Medium

Modern Blog Site with a Clean Interface
medium.com

There's something calming about the white background and black words of **Medium**, the blogging platform from the founder of Twitter. There are no themes, no blinking boxes, no busy columns. Medium has text and pictures and words and ideas. You write your piece, and the world can respond, even to a very specific area of your post. You can make collections of other content on your pages, and the most popular posts end up on the front page. Medium is simple, stark, beautiful and purposeful; and it seamlessly integrates into your social media world.

GROWTH/CAREER

Also Check Out...

Squarespace
Drag-and-Drop Website Builder
squarespace.com

Weebly
Site Builder with Added Features Like Email Marketing
weebly.com

Wix
Highly Customizable Online Site Builder
wix.com

Confession: I wrote under the WordPress description that starting a blog or website is easy. That's true, but setting up a professional site and making it do everything you want does have a learning curve with WordPress. The system is truly one of the most flexible and powerful, but it can be complicated.

For simple drag-and-drop sites, you can't beat **Squarespace**, **Weebly** and **Wix**. Wix is probably the best of the three because of ease of set up and hundreds of templates. With all these services, you should expect to pay a monthly fee for hosting and services. I've heard but can't verify that WordPress is better for SEO (search engine optimization), but perhaps that's selective reading on my part because I prefer WordPress.

NerdHerder Donna Mortensen loves the Squarespace blog capabilities. "Squarespace's Blog app lets me manage my blog on my iPad, wherever I am, without having to do it on a laptop. That's useful not just for adding posts on the go, but, more importantly, for approving or replying to comments in real time instead of having to wait until I can get to a full PC."

Organize and Synchronize Contacts

• •

My contact list is a big honkin' mess, full of duplicates, sloppiness and overall chaos. Don't be like me. Use these tools to get your contact list in line.

Start with...

FullContact
The Best Contact Management System on the Planet
fullcontact.com

Each and every time I have a discussion with attendees about contact management systems, **FullContact** is the top response. The system merges your duplicate contacts, even from different devices and platforms, keeping all your contact systems current no matter where they live. It also scans public data to keep you up to date with your contacts' latest photos, jobs and social profiles. When your contacts have a new signature line, FullContact updates the info in their profile.

A super feature of FullContact is its business card processing. Just snap pictures of cards, and FullContact's human people will transcribe them and add them to your list.

The free version gives you 1,000 contacts and the ability to sync with one other account. Plus, you get 10 business card transcriptions. The paid levels start with syncing to five accounts and 25,000 contacts.

And because so many of my attendees say it's the best thing out there, I would venture a guess that all these features will make your contact management a whole lot easier.

GROWTH/CAREER

Then Try...

Contactually
Contact Management with a Built-In Bucket Game
contactually.com

Nimble
Social Media-Connected Contact Management Tool
nimble.com

Although FullContact is mentioned most often by my community, **Contactually** and **Nimble** have special features that make them stand out. Contactually helps you sort your kabillion contacts into buckets by way of an amusing game of flicking them into literal buckets. And Nimble gets extra points because it not only connects your contacts via email, but it also searches out their social media posts to give you more of an idea of who they are and where they hang out online.

Also Check Out...

CamCard
Card Scanning App
camcard.com

Just like people love FullContact for contact management, they love **CamCard** to capture business cards for their contact lists. You just snap a picture of the card, verify the info, then add to your contacts. You can also exchange electronic cards with people.

Gotta tell ya… I've never been satisfied with automatic card readers. I just gave it another try with a couple of cards. One card was very basic, and CamCard nailed it. The second card was my husband's, which is black with a yellow stripe for his name (D.J. Rausa). After two tries, CamCard identified his full name as "The Law Of-Fices of."

Some of the fields came in just fine, but the company was "D.J.Rausa" (no spaces), and the department was "D. j. PAUSA." I don't have the time or patience to edit each line when the card is non-standard. So I use Fancy Hands (Page 160) to have humans do my data entry.

NerdHerd Thumbs Up: Conference Tools

iLeads

iSessions

Tools for Conferences

bartizan.com

Ordinarily I don't cover tools that say "contact us for pricing," but NerdHerder Chris Eisenberg works for the company that makes **iLeads** and **iSessions**, and he thinks they have earned a place in *The Big Book of Apps*.

From Chris:

iLeads allows exhibitors at trade shows to capture and qualify leads. iSessions allows show organizers to track attendance, with access control, CEU tracking and certificates and self-service scanning.

I know I work there, but seriously they are superior apps which do not get enough attention in the marketplace, especially iSessions which is unrivaled as a session tracking app.

Research Connections and Prospects

• •

When you're meeting with a prospective client, employer or just a new contact, you should take a few minutes to read through the company profile, the LinkedIn facts, recent news mentions and other interesting tidbits that will show your contact that you're paying attention.

But if you're like me, you will run out of time before you do your homework. Wouldn't it be nice if you had help with your research? Stay tuned….

Start with...

Charlie
Research Tool for Meeting Attendees
charlieapp.com

Connect your cloud-based calendar and contact lists to the **Charlie** app, and the system will search your calendar for upcoming meetings. An hour before the rendezvous, Charlie sends you a short email with publicly available info for your attendees and their companies. Charlie does the best research when you use the best email addresses. If you use a person's personal email address when her LinkedIn account uses the business, you're not going to get great results.

The paid version of Charlie is in a SalesForce plugin, which means that most of us can use the website and the iOS app for free.

Crystal   #CreepyButHelpful
Contact Research Tool that Analyzes Personalities
crystalknows.com

> Did you know that I respond well to emoticons in written communication?

> Or that I'd like to chat a little about this and that before we get down to business?

Or that you should schedule a meeting with me around food and drink?

Although I haven't spent that much time on self-analysis, it was no surprise to me that when a new service called **Crystal** analyzed my personality based on my online presence and writing, it declared that "Beth is social, creative, trusts feelings and gut instinct more than rules or logic, and loves talking about ideas."

Crystal is a creepy tool. It scours online profiles and returns recommendations for talking, writing and selling to our contacts. The system is set up to analyze online content and immediately categorize people using the DiSC® personality profiles. You can take a 10-question personality quiz to help it analyze your personality, and if you verify a relationship with someone, you can answer questions about others as well.

They've changed the pricing and the freebie offerings a few times, but as of this writing, you can analyze any of your contacts (including your LinkedIn connections) for free, or lookup anyone for a few bucks a month. The paid version includes the very valuable Gmail plugin, which analyzes contacts as they come into your email inbox and guides your email correspondence as you type.

Then Try...

Nudge
Contact Manager and Researcher
nudge.ai

I'm not sure if **Nudge** belongs in the contact management section (Page 185) or here. The system works with Gmail (Page 64) and Microsoft contact and email information to determine the strength of your online networks and the relationships among your contacts. It also finds news and updates about your contacts and their companies.

The real magic comes in with the Chrome Extension. Just hover over an email correspondent, and Nudge shows full contact info, a description of your relationship, recent company news, social media updates and more.

Note: When you connect your email to Nudge, be sure to add all your addresses as aliases. Otherwise it'll just look for relationships between your main Gmail or Microsoft account.

Hunter
Email Hunting Tool and More
hunter.io

Let's say you'd like to find someone at my company. You'd go to **Hunter** and enter my URL, and every publicly listed email address for people at our company will show up along with the source of the info. You can also verify email addresses and search a couple of different ways, including with browser extensions. You get 150 searches a month for free.

Also Check Out...

BatchGeo
Lead Mapping Tool
batchgeo.com

Google My Maps
Another Lead Mapping Tool
google.com/mymaps

Both **BatchGeo** and **Google My Maps** let you upload spreadsheets of your prospects or clients to see where they are and where they're not, giving you great insight into where you should focus your sales and marketing efforts. BatchGeo has some advanced features with the paid level, but Google My Maps is free, so....

NerdHerd Thumbs Up:
Article Research Tool

YouGotTheNews
Research Resource for Contact News
yougotthenews.com

YouGotBlogs
Research Resource for Contact Blog
  Mentions
yougotblogs.com

NerdHerder Sam Richter is a fellow speaker and one smart dude when it comes to researching contacts. He submitted **YouGotTheNews** as a place to discover newspaper articles about your contacts and other research topics. "I use this prior to meeting with prospects and clients to find news articles that are relevant to the other person. It's generally more comprehensive than Google News." Also check out **YouGotBlogs** for, well, blogs.

GROWTH/CAREER

Change a Habit

● ●

Want to stop smoking? Exercise more? Break your smartphone addiction? These tools help you start good habits or stop bad ones.

Start with...

Habitica
Gamified Habit-Forming Tool
habitica.com

If you're motivated by gold stars and "winning," **Habitica** may be for you. The system is set up like a video game where you conquer little monsters to meet daily goals and establish better habits. Along the way, you can earn "sweet gear" like an invaluable 8-bit sword or pixelated horned helmet. While the idea is clever, I think I'd be more motivated by earning digital cupcakes. Habitica lets you join forces with friends to hold each other accountable.

stickK
Habit-Building Tool with Community-Based Accountability
stickk.com

Another way to meet a goal is to make it public and find people to keep you accountable. A free site called **stickK** lets you set your goals via a Commitment Contract and pledge a private monetary commitment to your chosen "referee." Your referee has the last call on whether you met your goal; and if not, he (or a charity or other entity) will get the money.

Way of Life
Simple Habit Maker with Easy Updates
wayoflifeapp.com

People love the simple interface and easy update capabilities of **Way of Life**. I like the name because it reminds us that a new habit should be part of our daily lives.

Then Try...

BreakFree

Control Your Smartphone Addiction
breakfree-app.com

According to **BreakFree**, the average adult checks his phone 110 times a day. BreakFree should know, because the app tracks how often you check your phone to help you break the habit.

Google Goals

Google's Attempt to Work Good Habits into Your Schedule
In Google Calendar Mobile Apps

If you don't mind Google keeping track of your every move, you might like **Google Goals**, a feature inside Google Calendar on your mobile devices. The feature asks you what habit you want to make time for, such as working out more or spending more time with family. Then Google will search your calendar for open windows and blocks off time to help you meet your goal.

Also Check Out...

Unstuck

Interactive Goal-Setting Tool with Breakthrough Ideas
unstuck.com

When you have lapsed into inaction because you're stuck... it's time to get **Unstuck**. This beautifully designed tool walks you through questions about why you're not advancing at work, in your relationships or with personal goals. Then the system gives you exercises and ideas for overcoming your own objections and moving forward.

GROWTH/CAREER

Help Others

Much of today's technology is created to help ourselves, but some tools let you help others. These apps and sites make it easy to give back.

Start with...

Charity Miles
Fitness Tracking App that Raises Donations
charitymiles.org

If you're going to go for a run anyway, you can reap benefits beyond burning of the day's cupcake. **Charity Miles** is an app you use to choose a charity that will benefit from every mile you log running, walking or biking. The organization finds corporations to sponsor your activities. Since inception, they've donated more than $2M.

WoofTrax Walk for a Dog
Activity Tracker that Benefits Animal Shelters
wooftrax.com

Dogs need walks. Animal shelters need donations. Doesn't it make sense to link these two needs? **WoofTrax** thinks so. This app lets you turn your afternoon puppy outings into fundraising opportunities for your favorite shelters.

Donate a Photo

Johnson & Johnson App that Donates $1 for Every Photo You Share
donateaphoto.com

When you post photos on social media, you could be supporting your favorite charities if you use **Donate a Photo**. The app lets you share one photo per day to donate $1 to one of your favorite causes, courtesy of Johnson & Johnson.

Then Try...

Free Rice

A Vocabulary Builder with a Charity Twist
freerice.com

This site has long been one of my favorite ways to waste time online. Just take a vocabulary quiz (or math, or geography, or…), and for every question you get right, **Free Rice** gets a sponsor to donate 10 grains of rice to the World Food Programme to help end hunger.

Also Check Out...

Be My Eyes

App that Lets Sighted People See for the Visually Impaired
bemyeyes.com

Give the visually impaired a little help through **Be My Eyes**. Sighted volunteers receive notifications when someone needs their help to identify objects, read labels or discover colors. As of this book's printing, the Android app is still in the works.

Keep an Eye on My Online Reputation

When you meet new people, there's a good chance they're gonna Google you. Make sure you keep up with what info your contacts will find.

Start with...

Google Alerts
Free News Monitoring for Your Name and Brand
google.com/alerts

BrandYourself
Google Results Monitoring
brandyourself.com

If you are a professional, you need to be using **Google Alerts**. With Google Alerts, you can track keywords in the web world in news articles, blogs and other citations. Set them up for your company's name, your name, even hot keywords in your field. You will receive emails that list places your alerts were mentioned on the web.

I set them up for my last name, my company and keywords related to my clients. Every mention is aggregated and delivered via email. This saves me the hassle of doing "ego searches."

If your front-page Google results are less than desirable, **BrandYourself** can help. You can sign up for free monitoring and submit good sites (like your LinkedIn profile) so that your search results look more professional and are truly yours (not another Beth Ziesenis).

Then Try...

Rep'nUp
Social Media Scanner for Harmful Posts
repnup.com

If half your Instagram pics have you holding a beer, a prospective employer might think your priorities don't align with their values (or they could consider that a strength!). **Rep'nUp** scans your social media sites for posts that may be harmful to your professional image. When it scanned my Facebook page, the tool found where I wrote, "root canals suck" and one where I talked about heavy drinking in an airport bar. Bet you didn't know I was such a rebel!

You can earn subscriptions by inviting friends to sign up, or just pay a one-time fee of ten bucks. Or you could just accept that sometimes you're an idiot online like I do.

Also Check Out...

NameChk
Domain and Social Media Check for Your Brand
namechk.com

Believe it or not, the domain "http://nerdy.ninja" is still available. I know this because I searched **NameChk** for availability of domains, social media usernames and trademarks. The free site is a quick way to research your brand and acquire related sites and social media accounts to enrich your online presence.

GROWTH/CAREER

Focus and Get Things Done

• •

Research studies have proven over and over again that we as a society suck at multitasking. But turning everything off to focus on one task is a challenge in itself. That's where these tools come in.

Start with...

The Pomodoro Technique®
Kitchen Timer Productivity Technique
cirillocompany.de/pages/pomodoro-technique

FocusDots
Pomodoro-Type Time Management App
squrce.com/focusdots

Hands down this is the very best tool in my focus toolbox. **The Pomodoro Technique®** was created by an Italian guy named Francesco Cirillo with a tomato-shaped kitchen timer (*pomodoro* is Italian for "tomato"). He'd set the timer for 25 minutes and focus on ONE TASK... just ONE... for the entire 25 minutes. He'd block out calls, emails, dings, dongs and doorbells. When the timer went off, he'd take a 5-minute break to catch up on other things, then dive back into another 25-minute stretch.

The cool thing about the Pomodoro Technique is that you can do it with a kitchen timer, a fancy app or just the stopwatch on your phone. I have a couple of timers on my Mac. On my phone, I like **FocusDots**, which counts the number of focus sessions you have in a day. It's pretty—calming, almost—and helps you visualize all the tasks you've accomplished. But you don't have to use my recommendation. There are TONS of these apps. Just search "Pomodoro."

Then Try...

StayFocusd
Chrome Plugin for Site Blocking
nerdybff.com/stayfocusd-app

Forest
Focus Tool that Grows Trees
forestapp.cc

StayFocusd is the site-blocking app that kept me out of my email and off Facebook so I could write this book. This simple Chrome browser plugin that lets you set rules to restrict yourself from going to time-sucking sites. If you just want to stay away from your phone, you might download **Forest** (or add a web plugin). Open the tool and watch digital trees sprout and grow as long as you resist your forbidden technology. My manager, Molly, loves the app and enjoys adding to her forest. She's kind of a hippie. We love her for that.

Also Check Out...

RescueTime   #CreepyButHelpful
Software that Tracks Where the Time Goes
rescuetime.com

If you're constantly wondering, "Where did today go?", you might be ready for **RescueTime**. This software runs on your computer and keeps track of every second you spend on your device and every place you spend it. You'll see time reports for how long it took you to finish a document in Microsoft Word and how many minutes you spent surfing cool cupcake pictures on Pinterest. The free version is quite robust.

Health

I want to . . .

HEALTH

Wake Up in Style

· ·

My first alarm clock looked like the one in "Groundhog Day" with the flipping numerals and the static-y radio set to go off at 6 AM. Now most of us probably use our devices with about a billion options for ways to wake up.

Start with...

Sleep Time

Motion-Activated Sleep Monitor and Alarm

azumio.com/apps/sleep-time

The **Sleep Time** alarm is my favorite. You sleep with your phone next to you on the bed (but not under your pillow—some devices get blazing hot!), and it monitors your sleep cycle. When your alarm goes off, the app will gently wake you during a lighter cycle so you aren't jolted from a deep sleep.

Then Try...

Alarmy

Annoying Alarm Clock

alar.my

Alarmy calls itself the world's most annoying alarm clock, and I think it qualifies. Set alarms in three modes. One makes you get out of bed and take a picture of an object you've chosen. Another makes you shake the dang phone until you're wide awake. The third alarm option asks you to solve a math puzzle before the alarm stops sounding.

See? Annoying.

Wakie

#CreepyButHelpful

Creepy Alarm Clock

wakie.com

Wakie is a little weird—OK, maybe even creepy. This alarm app connects its users so that strangers give you your wake-up call. No one sees anyone else's phone number, but still. Weird. If no one is around to call you, it defaults to a regular alarm.

Also Check Out...

Alarm Clock for Me (iOS)

My Alarm Clock (Android)

Beautiful Nightstand Alarm Clock

apalon.com

Apalon makes beautiful alarm clocks for both Apple and Android devices. I'm not quite sure why they named them differently. Both have attractive interfaces, versatile alarms and weather updates.

Get Active

I ran my first marathon in 2007—and my sixth (and last) in 2012. I offer that as proof that at one time I knew what I was talking about when it comes to tools to help you stay active.

Start with...

Zombies, Run!

Running App with Zombies

zombiesrungame.com

7 Minute Superhero Workout

Short Workout Routines that Save the World

superheroworkoutgame.com

The app developer Six to Start has two of my favorite workout apps. I'm always partial to tools that begin with a Z, but I truly do love **Zombies, Run!** This was Six to Start's original fitness app. The game motivates you to lace up your running shoes with adventures and storylines around blood-thirsty zombies.

And the amusing **7 Minute Superhero Workout** takes you through short exercise challenges that will help you save the world.

Then Try...

MapMyFitness

Comprehensive Fitness Tracker
mapmyfitness.com

MapMyFitness is kind of an umbrella app for Under Armour's collection of fitness apps. You can use it to track any workout with any fitness app. If you're into more specialized workouts, such as cycling, you can try other apps in the series: **MapMyRide**, **MapMyRun**, **MapMyWalk** and **MapMyHike**. Under Armour also integrates its nutrition app, MyFitnessPal (Page 208).

Also Check Out...

Runtastic

Running, Cycling and Fitness GPS Tracker
runtastic.com

NerdHerder Cindy Camargo uses **Runtastic** for fitness tracking. "When going on a walk, you can gauge how far you've gone!" she says.

Seconds Interval Timer

Interval Timer App for HIIT, Tabata and
   Circuit Training
runloop.com/seconds-pro

Elizabeth Cogan should be my role model. This NerdHerder's favorite tool is **Seconds Interval Timer**, which helps you create intervals for hardcore workouts. Elizabeth says, "Seconds Interval Timer establishes a timer for different CrossFit activities." Good for you, Elizabeth! My workouts don't get any more stressful than hunting down Pokémon.

Sworkit

Workout Videos for a Custom Fitness Program

sworkit.com

One of my biggest excuses for not working out is that I'm always on the road. **Sworkit** takes away that roadblock. (Get it? On the road with roadblocks? Ha!) by offering exercise plans that can be done anywhere for any length of time without any equipment. Easy-to-follow videos walk you through a workout. The paid version provides access for you to create unlimited custom workouts and offers more fine tuning.

Hot Topics:
Wearables

As far as I'm concerned, the Apple Watch is still a *want*, not yet a *need* for most of us. Although I enjoy the capability to quickly see my incoming texts and sometimes use it for travel, the primary purpose so far has been to track my activity. And with the $270+ price tag, it's way more expensive than other fitness wearables.

NerdHerder Gloria Rossiter loves her **Fitbit** (fitbit.com), which has a line of devices that start at about $60 and tops off at $200. Gloria likes the collaboration feature. "Competition with others keeps me motivated to exercise."

Watch What I Eat

•••

Ok, folks. If you're reading my book to find out my take on the best app for dieting, you obviously didn't pay attention to my picture on the cover. But I'm ok with a do-as-I-say-not-as-I-do approach to this category if you are.

Start with...

Lark
AI Nutrition Coach
web.lark.com

I always thought that if I just had a nutrition coach peering over my shoulder as I ate to help me make better choices, I'd be miraculously transformed into a size 6.

Turns out having a nutrition coach on demand is just irritating to me.

Lark is an app that uses artificial intelligence to evaluate your food intake and keep you on track. It's ~~judgy and unforgiving~~ knowledgeable and encouraging as you use natural language to chat with the ~~know-it-all~~ science-based chatbot advisor. The 16-week programs are designed to give you a good start on better habits. So try it. Or not. $20 a month.

Then Try...

MyFitnessPal
Calorie and Activity Tracker
myfitnesspal.com

Lose It!
Calorie and Activity Tracker with
  Food Image Recognition
loseit.com

Of these two apps, **MyFitnessPal** is the most well known and perhaps the most beloved. Under Armour bought it in 2017, expanding its extensive reach even further. The app integrates into the very popular fitness series named MapMy… Ride, Fitness, Run, Walk, etc. (Page 205), as well as many other fitness trackers and other wellness tools. NerdHerder Doris Nurenberg says, "MyFitnessPal has helped me be aware of what I am eating and learn a balance for future health. It goes with me everywhere (via smartphone) and is very easy to use."

Lose It! also has many fans, but it's the Snap It! feature that makes it stand out, at least in theory. You snap a picture of your meal, and the app uses image recognition to determine what you're eating and how much. I gave it a try in early 2017, and it needs improvement. It identified my egg as an almond and my kale/steak combo as macaroni and cheese.

Also Check Out...

MakeMyPlate
Visual-Based Meal Planner and Calorie Tracker
makemyplate.co

For those of us who still believe that a quart of Ben & Jerry's is one serving, there's **MakeMyPlate**. This app helps you visualize healthy meals with pictures on a virtual plate.

NerdHerd Thumbs Up:
Make Restaurant Reservations

OpenTable
Restaurant Reservation Tool
opentable.com

If you're tired of counting calories and just want a great place to eat, Bill Soellner recommends **OpenTable**, an app that helps you discover new restaurants and make reservations. And why is this Bill's favorite tool? "I love to eat well," he says. I'm with ya, Bill.

Stay Calm

• •

Family… work… money… relationships… stressors in any one of these areas can affect the others. Be proactive with managing stress and anxiety with these tools that help you chill out.

Start with...

Noisli
Background Noise Tool
noisli.com

I have a very tough time working in complete silence—something has to be on in the background. These days I usually have a small tablet tuned to reruns of "Matlock," but if you don't have that option, just pull up the **Noisli** site for sounds that will help you get stuff done. You can click on a pre-programmed Productivity button to hear birds chirping and a gentle creek flowing, or you can fine-tune the sounds by clicking around the icons. I like the sounds of a coffee shop mixed with the rain.

Then Try...

Calm
Meditation Tool for Online and on the Go
calm.com

Headspace
Another Meditation Tool
headspace.com

You don't need a zafu pillow and a Buddha statue to meditate. Just pull out an app. **Calm** and **Headspace** are both popular meditation tools that guide you through quick mindfulness exercises no matter where you are. Both have free options as well as a subscription service.

Also Check Out...

Gratitude Apps

I was inspired to try a gratitude journal app after listening to a fantastic speaker named Mary C. Kelly (who is also a member of the NerdHerd!). She talked about changing your attitude in several different ways. One that struck me as the easiest was to swap out the phrase" have to" for "get to," as in:

- *What I used to think*: I have to go to work.

  What Mary taught me to think: I get to go to work and do something I love while making a living for myself and my family.

- *What I used to think*: I have to do the dishes.

  What Mary taught me to think: I get to do the dishes with a modern dishwasher in my beautiful home. I'm so fortunate to have these amenities.

- *What I used to think*: I have to go on a diet.

  What Mary taught me to think: I get to change my eating habits to become more happy and healthy.

Just that simple switch makes all the difference.

There are lots of gratitude journal apps for your mobile devices. I'm not particularly in love with the one I chose, so I won't bother with a review. I don't even remember the name. But the premise is the same: every day you *get to* share things you're grateful about. And I love that there's no place for a "but."

Special Guest Star: Molly's Mindfulness Tips

My manager, Molly Gardner, is one of the most chill people I know. I asked her to share her wisdom about technology that helps you stay calm. Also check out her top 10 list of tools that help her at work on Page 30.

Technology equals the future, right? The next best thing. Tomorrow's trend. A new generation of ideas. The future is bright (and we love our tech tools!) but there is a need for technology and rules that keep us in the present moment, nurturing today's important ideas and communicating richly with our teams and clients. That's where mindfulness comes into play.

1. **Install a Time Management App**

   RescueTime (Page 199) tracks the time you spend on projects and websites. Block time-sucking websites and receive a daily or weekly report of where you spent your time.

2. **Get Focused... Realistically**

   Taking breaks is an important part of staying mindful and focused. Pomodoro is a productivity technique: work for 25 minutes and take a 5-minute break. Letting your mind wander for a short period will help you train your brain to stay focused on the task at hand for a full 25-minutes of genuine work. **Pomodoro.cc** is a simple (and free) web-based tool that doesn't even require a login. Or, if you like to keep a timer on your mobile device or as a plugin, **Pomodoro One** (Page 198) and **Forest** (Page 199) are good options.

3. **Find the Right Task Manager**

   The most important part of maintaining mindfulness in business and in life is the ability to focus on today. A task manager will help you to decipher what needs to get accomplished today and what is tomorrow's challenge. I sing praises to **Todoist** (Page 7) on a daily basis, but it doesn't matter which task management tool you use. Throw out the sticky notes and find an online task manager that works for you. The right task manager enables you to turn a non-crucial email into next week's task. Add a note for your summer project and share it with your team. Start your day reviewing the tasks on hand... maybe some of them are no longer in tune with your goals or can be best addressed another time.

4. Outsource Small Tasks

Part of being mindful is making choices about what we can accomplish in a day. Make a list of all the tasks you do in a day or a week. If you were to pass off small tasks would it help you to stay present for your business and your family? Consider letting **Fancy Hands** (Page 160) handle your son's birthday party plans or compare local dentists. Outsource a marketing project to **Fiverr** (Page 160) rather than wrestling with Photoshop. Let go of the projects that keep you from where you are most valuable.

5. Find Some Quiet

Download **Noisli** (Page 210) to block out hectic office noise with the soothing sounds designed to help you focus. And make the most of those new 5-minute breaks with a quick meditation courtesy of **Calm**.

6. Turn Off Your Tech

There. I said it. Turn off your text alerts and shut down your inbox. This idea is almost heresy at Nerd HQ but hear me out. Technology is there to serve us, not vice-versa. Do what works for you. Make it a rule to work in the mornings and check email after lunch.

Focus on today's opportunity to create meaningful work. Be present with today's people and projects. Take joy in each task you do... even the mundane can be enjoyable when you pay attention.

HEALTH

Step Away from the Computer

When smoking in the office became taboo, the tobacco addicts took work breaks to huddle together in the smoking alcove outside.

If one looked to find any kind of benefit from the smoke breaks, it was the fact that these workers left their desks to walk around every few hours. These days many of us park ourselves in front of our monitor when the workday begins and only move for bathroom breaks or to sweep by the desk of the wonderful person who always keeps candy in a jar.

Today people who nag you about your health say sitting is the new fettuccini Alfredo. Sitting all day at a desk can cause spine curvature, carpel tunnel syndrome, eye strain and a multitude of problems with your heart health and overall fitness. The health detriments add insult to injury because chances are you're stuck at your computer surrounded by stress and trying to keep up with the crazy pace of our crazy busy lives.

But fear not! From the early years of web apps, developers have offered tools to help you remember to sit up straight and take regular breaks. Here are a handful of tools and gadgets that help us.

Start with...

Regular Breaks
Site that Traps Your Curser Until You Take a Break
regularbreaks.com

From the maker of one of my favorite older tools, Big Stretch by MonkeyMatt.com (ok, it may be that I love it just for his name), we have **Regular Breaks**, a web app that forces you to take breaks while you're working away.

Move It
Activity Break Tool
thepegeekapps.com/moveit

This one's made for teachers to help students get moving, but it also works for the office. **Move It** helps you take breaks with exercises designed to get your heartrate up for brief intervals. It's an iOS app or Windows download, but you can use it with Chrome as well.

Then Try...

PYV
Site that Gives Your Eyes a Break
protectyourvision.org

Protectyourvision.org offers a cool little web app with this adorable mascot that focuses on giving your eyes a break. I'm a little concerned that the page hasn't been updated in a while, but the nerdy cartoon makes me love it.

Also Check Out...

F.lux
Computer Lighting Adjustment Tool
justgetflux.com

My (completely awesome) former assistant Claire Parrish stumbled upon this tool: **f.lux** adapts the lighting level of your computer's display to the time of day, such as warm at night and like sunlight during the day. After staring 8 hours at your screen, you'll appreciate the mellow and adjusting light.

HEALTH

Hot Topic:
How Can Gadgets Help
Keep Me Moving?

Lumoid
Device Tryer-Outer
lumoid.com

Today's wearables have built-in motion sensors that can nudge you when you've been sitting too long. My Apple Watch clanks me every hour to remind me to stand and be active for one minute, and if I do it 12 times in one day, I receive praise and sometimes even a badge. Silly as that sounds, it does motivate me to move from my computer and celebrate when I "win."

Of course, the Apple Watch is a pretty pricey toy as an activity monitor, so you might try other fitness trackers, many of which run less than a hundred bucks. Don't know which one to use? Check out **Lumoid** to try them out three at a time for a small fee so you can determine which one you want.

You can also find gadgets to help with your posture. UpRight and Lumo Lift sense when you start slouching and remind you to sit up. Darma does it with a seat cushion. Boy do I need one of those!

Stay Healthy

● ●

Technology has given us many options for monitoring, improving and reporting on our health. As always, check with your personal healthcare provider and insurance folks to make sure these are the best resources for your needs.

Start with...

Doctor On Demand

Virtual Doctors for Physical and Mental Health
doctorondemand.com

I'm sure you've heard about tele-medicine, where the doctors and nurses literally "phone it in" when it comes to healthcare, offering services via phone and video conferencing.

A participant told an amazing story about **Doctor On Demand**. She was on an extended business trip when she caught strep throat, which she had contracted many times before. A friend recommended that she download Doctor On Demand, which lets you connect to general physicians, pediatricians, mental health professionals and more. Within minutes of downloading the app and registering, she was talking to a verified physician via video. The doctor asked her to point the camera toward her throat, quizzed her about symptoms and agreed with her self diagnosis.

Within an hour of downloading the app, she was on her way to the airport with a stop at a pharmacy to get the prescription she needed.

The cost of a "visit" starts at $40, and some insurances will cover the services. You can also schedule calls with mental health professionals for counseling or medication, and they have specialists for children and pregnant patients.

HEALTH

Then Try...

CareZone
Record Keeper for Your Family's Health
carezone.com

CareZone is an app that organizes your medical information—it's as easy as scanning your prescriptions into the app. CareZone then alerts you about refills and helps remind you to take your pills. What's more, you can keep track of other people's prescriptions and health info—a wonderful feature for those of us who are keeping tabs on elderly parents or kids.

GoodRx
Pill Identifier and Prescription Price Comparisons
goodrx.com

GoodRx helps you identify pills and understand their effects, but the best feature is the comparison tool that searches the prices of your prescription at area pharmacies and lets you know where it'll be cheapest.

iTriage
Health Monitoring and Symptom Reference Guide
itriagehealth.com

Perhaps the world is a more dangerous place now that we can Google every strange bump that appears on our body. But since we're going to self-diagnose anyway, we might as well have the right information. **iTriage** helps you identify symptoms and figure out the right questions to ask your healthcare providers. You can also keep all your medical records together and monitor medications. The app even connects you with medical facilities to make appointments and find specialists.

AskMD
Medical Care and Follow Up
sharecare.com/static/askmd

You Google what could be causing your hacking cough. Wouldn't it be nice if someone followed up in a few days to see if you're doing better? **AskMD/Sharecare** does just that.

Hot Topic:
Apps for the Greater Good

Child Protector
Child Injury Assessment Tool
childrensmercy.org/childprotector

TraffickCam
Web App to Fight Sex Trafficking
traffickcam.com

My brilliant college roommate, Dr. Raquel Vargas-Whale, is a child abuse expert. She recommended the **Child Protector** app for both child care professionals and lay people. The app assesses the risk that a finding or situation represents maltreatment and gives a plan of action. "It's a good teaching tool with helpful animations," she says.

Another easy-to-use app that may help victims of sex trafficking is the **TraffickCam** site, which lets ordinary travelers like you and me upload photos of your hotel rooms. The photos are added to a searchable database to help sex trafficker investigators identify locations of trafficking activity.

Photo and Video

....

I want to . . .

PHOTO/VIDEO

Use Image Filters and Auto-Art Tools

When it comes to drawing and art, I'm a great caption writer. But I can fake talent with the numerous image creation and editing tools that can create artsy effects for digital images.

Here's a list of my favorite artsy tools. Check out the NerdHerd members that show off what these things can do.

Art Effects

Photofy
Advanced Photo Editor with Filters and Stickers
photofy.com

Not only does **Photofy** add cool stickers and filters, it also is a heavy-duty photo editor that can make your image look more professional.

PicsArt
Do-It-All Image Editor
picsart.com

I love Prisma for its simple interface, but **PicsArt** may be the most versatile tool. It has filters, drawing tools, collage features, creative brushes and more goodies.

Prisma
Photo App that Transforms Images into
    Works of Art with AI
prisma-ai.com

Count me among the thousands (millions?) of people around the world who have fallen in love with **Prisma**. The app transforms your photos and even video clips into artworks

Kimberly Lilley in Prisma

using the styles of famous artists. The images are as filtered as a filter can be, and it takes an ordinary snapshot and makes it special.

#NerdPartyTrick

AutoDraw
AI Drawing Tool
autodraw.com

You will be unstoppable in Pictionary if you use **AutoDraw**. The site uses artificial intelligence to interpret your chicken-scratch drawing, instantly converting your circle with two triangles to the cat face you wanted to draw.

Text Effects

Stencil
Instant Text-Over-Image Tool with
Chrome Plugin
getstencil.com

You guys probably know how much I adore Canva (Page 248), the graphic design tool that lets you make graphics for almost every possible scenario: social media, resumes, business cards and much more. **Stencil**, formerly known as Save As Image, revamped itself to be more Canva-like and offers access via a site or browser plugin.

Diana Hersch in Stencil

Although Stencil can't compete with Canva price-wise or in the sheer number of templates, Stencil has a special feature that makes it handy. Highlight a great quote or phrase on any website then use the browser plugin button to transform that text into an image that you can place on any background.

PHOTO/VIDEO

Tagxedo
Word Cloud Maker
tagxedo.com

Tagxedo by Beth Bridges

Tagxedo is my very favorite word cloud tool because of its flexibility. You can make a quick, traditional word collage in less than 5 minutes, or create a perfect masterpiece with umpteen customizations.

To use Tagxedo, like many word art sites, you upload a list of words, or the tool will analyze a document, site or pasted text. Depending on your settings, the most frequent words in your text will appear larger than the other words.

Note: Tagxedo is an online-only web app that doesn't work on mobile devices or Chrome browsers because it runs on an older technology called Microsoft Silverlight. Try it in Firefox.

WordFoto

iOS App that Paints Pictures
  with Words

wordfoto.com

Typo Effect Photo Editor

Android App that Paints
  Pictures with Words

typographydesign.in

I swore that I wouldn't
include a one-platform app
in the book, but I can't help
myself. **WordFoto** is so
much fun. It's an old app
that hasn't been updated in
a while, but I love the
effects. Google Play's **Typo
Effect Photo Editor** is kind
of like WordFoto. Kind of.

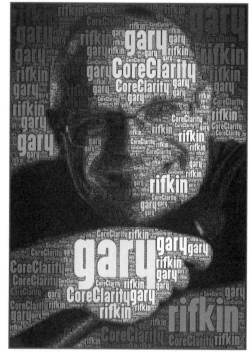

Gary Rifkin in WordFoto

NerdHerd Thumbs Up:
A Photo Editing App

Snapseed
Image Tools and Filters
snapseed.com

The **Snapseed** app from Google is both powerful and
popular, and NerdHerder Jeremy Shugars loves it.
"Snapseed is a simple yet powerful tool for quality photo
editing on the go. From simple tuning to adding text,
Google has developed yet another winner."

Frame Effects

Pho.to
Image Editing for Fun
    Frames, Filters and Editing
pho.to

Karyn Buxman in Pho.to

Photofacefun
My Favorite Photo Frame
    Site
photofacefun.com

Jeff Horn in PhotoFaceFun

If you need your face on the cover of a magazine or hanging in an art gallery, head over to these sites. I love these for quick graphics for my blog and newsletter.

Collages

EasyMoza
Photo Mosaic Site
easymoza.com

Picture Mosaics
Photo Mosaic Site with App
picturemosaics.com

Mozaikr
My Favorite Mosaic App (iOS)
mozai.kr

These three tools all do basically the same thing: create an image out of a whole bunch of other little images. **EasyMoza** and **Picture Mosaics** are both web based (Picture Mosaics has an app). Pick a main photo then a whole bunch of other photos to fill it. You can connect to Facebook, Instagram and other photo repositories for your images. Both sites allow you download and share low-res versions. EasyMoza sells the high-res files for up to $10. Picture Mosaics sells prints for a whole lot more.

Even though **Mozaikr** is only on Apple phones, I find it the easiest, fastest and free-est.

PicPlayPost
Video Postcards to Jazz Up Marketing
mixcord.co/partners/picplaypost.html

Putting **PicPlayPost** in the category of collages is doing it a disservice. Sure, you can make great photo collages with just a few clicks. But its secret sauce is the capability to make some of the images in your collage out of videos and GIFs. The end result is what I would consider a video postcard that makes a great social media post.

PHOTO/VIDEO

Avoid Paying for Photoshop

It's a well-known fact that if you need to crop an ex-boyfriend out of the family Christmas picture, your best option is Adobe Photoshop. The software used to be hundreds of dollars, but with Adobe's Creative Cloud monthly subscription, you can get it for about 10 bucks a month. NerdHerder Eileen Blake calls Photoshop "very versatile and reasonably priced." But even though Adobe tools are now in the realm of affordable, free is better.

Start with...

GIMP
The Original Free Photoshop Replacement
gimp.org

Pixlr
Online Photoshop Competitor
pixlr.com

GIMP, which stands for GNU Image Manipulation Program, was created in the mid-1990s and might be the king when it comes to open-source Adobe Photoshop competitors. Today a community of GIMP enthusiasts work together to upgrade the program, release new versions and get the word out. Download GIMP to manipulate photos with its many plug-ins and extensions, and visit the forums for lively and informative conversations about tips and bug fixes. Well, lively conversations for nerds.

Although GIMP has been around the longest, **Pixlr** is my favorite online image editor, with a Flash-based uploader that enables you to edit from any computer without software. From the Pixlr homepage, you can choose from three Pixlr online products. Pixlr's Express version is perfect for easy, immediate editing. It also has a fun Instagram-type filter and morphing tool, Pixlr-o-matic, which you can get online and on smart devices.

Pixlr Editor has many of the same features as Photoshop. All the tools you don't know how to use in Photoshop, you won't be able to figure out here either. It's that good.

Cool Update: 123RF (Page 245) purchased Pixlr in the spring of 2017, so I expect it to be around for some time and for 123RF to provide access to use the editing tools while you're organizing your images.

Then Try...

Adobe Photoshop Express

Adobe's Lightweight Photoshop Tool
photoshop.com/products/photoshopexpress

Adobe Photoshop Express may be just the lightweight image editor you need. You can launch a simple online editor from the site, or download the free apps. Then you can apply filters, borders and stickers, or crop, resize and fine-tune an image.

Also Check Out...

Inkscape

Vector Editor
inkscape.org

For advanced printing projects, you may need a more robust tool. Most digital graphic files are sized to look great on the screen but aren't high-enough resolution to print well at a decent size. That's why your designer for a print project will often ask for vector files, which can be increased in size without loss of quality, instead of JPEGs, which can't.

Inkscape is a free open-source vector editor and is considered a worthy competitor for Adobe Illustrator. Don't even ask me how to use it—Inkscape is way beyond my humble graphic skills.

PHOTO/VIDEO

PicMonkey

Lightweight Image-Editing Tool with Advanced Capabilities
picmonkey.com

Sometimes the advanced tools in Pixlr confuse me, and I just need to put a Santa hat on my avatar and move on with my life. **PicMonkey** is an easy-to-use online image tool with templates, stickers, fun fonts and filters.

As with Canva (Page 248), PicMonkey has many user-friendly tools to resize, revamp and re-engineer a graphic in minutes. You can also find helpful tools to make your teeth whiter and add a little color to your cheeks. (I haven't seen anything out there that automatically eliminates extra chins. Let me know if you find one.)

And if you need to layer graphics and do a little more advanced editing, you can find the tools to do so without needing a user's manual. PicMonkey has a robust free version that is supported with ads; or you can upgrade for $33 per year for no ads and more effects, fonts and other goodies. It calls its upgrade the Royale level, and the little monkey gets a crown. I'm a sucker for that cute stuff.

Vectr

Another Vector Editor
vectr.com

Although Inkscape is the best-known Adobe Illustrator replacement, check out **Vectr**, a tool that design experts praise for its easier interface and fast learning curve.

Print Photos and Albums

Whether you're creating a professional book with product images for work or a family album to treasure forever, these photo book services make the process easy and the product memorable.

Start with...

Felt

Accordion-Style Greeting Card from Your Phone
feltapp.com

Ever since **Felt** started offering a $5 subscription service, I've been a much better friend. For $5 a month, I can send up to three four-paneled Felt cards (including shipping). I use them for everything from a client thank-you to a husband I-love-you. They have amusing special occasions, such as Ellen DeGeneres' birthday and a lovely sentiment that says, "Dearest coworker, sorry about my stinky lunch." The cards are beautiful, and their square shape makes them hip (as in "it's hip to be square").

Then Try...

Groovebook

Monthly Photo Albums for $2.99
groovebook.com

I've talked before about things you can do with cool photos from your mobile devices, but one of my favorite projects is to turn phone photos into keepsake albums for a few dollars and with even fewer clicks. For **Groovebook**, just choose up to 100 photos per month, and once a month you'll receive an adorable little book with perforated 4x6" photos to share—for just $2.99 per month, including shipping. The price is so low that I have to double-check it every time I talk about it. Yep. It's just $2.99 still.

PHOTO/VIDEO

Chatbooks
A Fancier Monthly Photo Album
chatbooks.com

As much as I like the idea of Groovebook, I think the product is a little casual for use at the office. **Chatbooks** is more expensive but ever so much cuter. Choose 60 photos a month for a 5x5" book. A soft-cover subscription is $8, or $13 for a very impressive hardcover.

Mosaic
Deluxe Photo Album with Mosaic Cutout Cover
heymosaic.com

Mosaic's beautiful hardcover photo album is a bit pricy at $25, but it's an elegant way to showcase 20 phone pictures in a gift-ready package. The name comes from the mosaic look of the beautiful peek-a-boo cover.

Also Check Out...

Postagram
Photo Postcards from Your Phone
sincerely.com/postagram

You can find a whole bunch of apps that let you send real mail from your mobile device. With super-thick postcards with a picture that pops out, **Postagram** is my favorite. In the spring of 2017 they doubled the price per card from about a buck to just under two bucks. Sad face. But I still like 'em. So does NerdHerder Maggie who uses it for her "For Sale by Owner" business to connect with potential clients.

Create Videos and Multimedia

• •

In the early days of social media, gurus proclaimed, "Video is king!" Here we are almost 15 years after the founding of MySpace, and the sentence is still true. If you're not making videos to share your content, you're not engaging people to see your content.

Start with...

Animoto

Multimedia Photo and Video Montage Creator

animoto.com

Animoto takes your photos and short videos and synchronizes them into a multimedia movie complete with a soundtrack. Gather 10 or more pictures and/or videos, throw in a title and choose a theme and soundtrack—then push a button. PRESTO! Animoto instantly creates a perfectly timed, perfectly professional, perfectly awesome video that can showcase your event, your boss's retirement, your kid's prom preparations, your company's products—you name it.

The most versatile paid version is just $30 a year and gives you all kinds of extra functionality. Important note: Get a membership via the app, and you can use the app and the web to create and access videos. The pricing on the web is higher. (Weird, right? Don't ask me.)

You know who else loves Animoto? My NerdHerd friends! Pam Cochran says Animoto is easy to use "and the results are awesome." Vicki Glardon says making videos is fun, easy and quick. And Diana Hersch says, "It is efficient, fun, and captivating—AND done in seconds. Oh, AND FREE! Leaves your audience begging to learn how you did that. Nerdacious enough to warrant a five-star rating!"

PHOTO/VIDEO

Magisto

Movie Maker for Video Clips
magisto.com

Although **Magisto** doesn't have nearly the number of options as Animoto, this app does a great job with video clips and makes a cool instant movie. Just upload one or more video clips, and the tool uses smart editing to highlight snippets and apply filters and special effects. Try it out with the free version, or get extra options starting at $30 a year. The professional level enables you to do cool things with voiceovers.

Then Try...

Adobe Spark Video

Easy Voice-Over Video Tool
spark.adobe.com

Adobe Spark Video is one of the tools Adobe released as part of a service they call Spark. Find photos or upload your own on the web app or your iOS tablet Adobe. Then you record voiceovers for each slide in an incredibly easy process. After you have your video, you can change the theme and add a soundtrack. If you've used the images or music that Adobe provides, the tool will add the artist credits.

The bummer about Adobe Spark Video is that you can't download the video, so you'll have to play it online.

Also Check Out...

PowToon
Whiteboard Video Tool
powtoon.com

VideoScribe
Downloadable Whiteboard Video Tool
videoscribe.co

PowToon is a pioneer in low-cost whiteboard generators, which can cost thousands of dollars through a design firm. The online tool lets you start with templates to create presentations and videos. It takes a little finagling to get used to the interface; but when you understand the basics, you can create a brag-worthy showstopper. You can create PowToon-branded videos and slides for free, or buy a subscription starting at $19 per month for an annual plan. You can also keep the free version and just pay a few bucks to upgrade your video to HD.

One of my clients made an incredibly impressive whiteboard video using **VideoScribe**, which you can download on your computer or use on an iOS device. The pricing is about the same as PowToon, and the animations are a little more hand-drawn. Either tool makes you look like a pro.

PHOTO/VIDEO

Hot Topic:
Video Captions

Clips
Video Editor with Easy Captions
apple.com/clips

You may have noticed that many of the videos in your Facebook feed these days have captions. There's a good reason for this. Turns out most of us surf our social media sites at work, and we don't want blaring audio to give us away. So marketers have learned that if the videos don't have captions, they don't get seen.

Facebook makes captions easy. Just upload your video and go back in to edit. You'll see options for adding captions, aided by Facebook's auto-transcription. YouTube has similar capabilities. And Apple's **Clips** app will transcribe your video as you're speaking, giving you instant captions.

Edit Video and Audio

• •

From time to time all of us need to add a title to a video, trim a clip or join two segments into one movie. These downloads put the power of video editing into your hands. Two warnings: 1) there's a little bit of a learning curve for us non-designer types, and 2) they take up a lot of computing power and tons of storage space.

Start with...

iMovie
Apple Video Editor
apple.com/imovie

If you're playing around with homemade videos, you have to play with **iMovie**. The iOS app and Mac software include easy-to-use transitions, templates and treatments to turn raw videos into polished segments.

My favorite iMovie trick is to use one of the "coming attractions" templates to create what looks like a movie trailer. The templates tell you *exactly* what to shoot, with segment titles such as "Group" and "Two Shot" and "Action Shot." I made a superhero princess video with my little cousin in about 15 minutes, and it took me just 45 minutes to do one with my cats (their names are Copy and Paste). The little girl took direction much better than my kitties. The mobile app has fewer templates than the Mac version, but it's super cool to be able to create an entire video from your phone in minutes.

Lightworks
Award-Winning Video Editor
lwks.com

Although Windows Movie Maker is still kicking around as a download, Microsoft discontinued it in early 2017. Luckily **Lightworks** has a free version that even professional editors love. The software is available for Windows, Mac and Linux.

PHOTO/VIDEO

Then Try...

Audacity
Open-Source Audio Recorder and Editor
audacityteam.org

Amper Music
Make Your Own Soundtrack
ampermusic.com

Perhaps one of the best free downloadable tools that I almost never use is **Audacity**. It's a fully functional, incredibly professional, easy-to-use, multilingual audio editor and recorder. It's been around for as long as I've been seeking free stuff. Audacity doesn't have an app—just download it on your computer and edit like a pro.

If you need a background track, check out **Amper Music's** website. You can choose from a variety of styles and music moods then tweak until the snippet matches your video's theme and tone.

Also Check Out...

CyberLink PowerDirector
Community-Recommended Video Editor
cyberlink.com

When we put out a call for the best video editor recommendations, several in our nerdy community gave a thumbs up to **CyberLink PowerDirector**. The price is about $70 for the latest version, and everyone seems to love it.

Try Out Augmented Reality

The augmented reality game Pokémon Go put AR into focus for the masses in the summer of 2016. But we've actually had plenty of augmented reality tools at our disposal for many years, making it possible for you to embed bonus content into printed material with a few clicks.

Start with...

Layar
My Favorite Augmented Reality Tool
layar.com

For my second book (2013), I used **Layar** to create a graphic that you could scan for a video from me, bonus updates and a link to my site. The system is kind of like a QR code on steroids, where you use the app to scroll over an image for extra info. To make your own, you just upload an image then drag/drop media and info you want the scan to reveal, such as your Twitter feed, a video, or a push-to-call button with your contact information. You can add a Layar feature to your logo, postcard, business card and more. As soon as you save your Layar, the image is scannable by anyone with the app.

The cost is minimal per image, less than five bucks for one or less if you buy a bundle. But the biggest challenge is that people must have the app and know what to do with it. I found the conversion rate pretty low, just like QR codes, which never caught on.

Then Try...

Aurasma   #NerdPartyTrick
Another Augmented Reality Tool
aurasma.com

Like Layar, **Aurasma** lets you create your own "Auras" and even gives you fun little figures that you can embed in things you see. But my favorite Aurasma trick is to open the app and scroll over the back of a $1 or $20 bill. Again... a great nerdy party trick.

Also Check Out...

Blippar
Augmented Reality Tool with Facial Recognition
blippar.com

Blippar bought Layar, so I expect they'll be combining their brands one day. Blippar is one of the few stand-alone augmented reality tools that I've seen on other brands, as in "Download Blippar to view." Many of the other brands are incorporating the Blippar technology into their own apps.

As soon as you open Blippar, your view-   #CreepyButHelpful
finder will start recognizing things around
you. Blippar's cool twist is that it's working on facial recognition, which may soon evolve into you being able to scan a colleague and see information about him above his head. As of this writing, the facial recognition is generally limited to famous-ish people. I tried one of those a while ago, and it identified me as Arnold Schwarzenegger. So I am not really excited to give it another try.

Design

I want to . . .

DESIGN

241

Discover New Fonts

· ·

When it comes to the look and feel of a document, changing the font can change the personality, and it's easy to find free fonts to download and use.

Start with...

Dafont

Free Font Site with Interactive Preview Feature

dafont.com

Dafont is my very favorite place on the web to find fonts with pizazz to add a little something extra to a look. The key to finding your perfect font on Dafont is to put sample text into the custom preview box and then search by theme (cartoon, curly, calligraphy, handwritten). Most are free for personal use, and many are just plain free. Use filters to find ones you can use commercially. Read the fine print on fonts you use for work because the guidelines for use vary greatly.

Then Try...

Font Squirrel

Free Fonts for Commercial Use

fontsquirrel.com

Font Squirrel is another great resource, though it doesn't provide a preview of your text. The cool thing about the resources on this site is that they're all free for commercial use, so you won't have the letdown of finding the perfect font and then having to give it up because it's only for personal use.

Google Web Fonts

Font Sets for Online Use
google.com/fonts

If you're looking to add a little snazziness to your website, you can find new fonts that will work on the web at **Google Web Fonts**.

Also Check Out...

Wordmark.it

Preview Site for Fonts on Your Computer
wordmark.it

Have you ever spent a half-hour in Microsoft Word scrolling through your installed fonts one by one to find the perfect look for a document? **Wordmark.it** is a clever web tool that lets you write a few words for a preview then loads your fonts into the site so you can see them all at once. The site makes it easy for you to choose your favorites then filter them to see your top choices together. It's 100% free and super easy to use.

Find Royalty-Free Images and Multimedia
. . . .

Way back in the day, when small-business folks like me needed a nice image for our blogs, marketing or other stuff, we were forced to either, umm, "borrow" an image we found on the web (which was often low-resolution, thus bad for printing) or pony up hundreds for royalty-free stock photography from high-end sites such as Getty Images (Page 247).

But nowadays, there's no end to the number of so-called microstock sites—online marketplaces where freelance photographers and multimedia artists, both amateur and professional, sell their images for a fraction of the cost at the high-end sites.

We're also fortunate that talented artists and image curators offer many royalty-free images for the best price of… free.

Start with...

Everypixel
Multi-Site Image Search Engine
everypixel.com

One of the frustrations with finding the perfect image is that you have to search on approximately a thousand sites. **Everypixel** solves that problem for you by aggregating both free and paid microstock sites into one search engine. When an image is on multiple sites, Everypixel gives you prices so you can find the best bargain. #savemoney #savetime… #win!

Paid Sites

123RF
My Favorite Microstock Site
123rf.com

Adobe Stock
Subscription-Based Microstock Site that Integrates
into Adobe Products
stock.adobe.com

Dreamstime
Reasonably Priced Photos
dreamstime.com

Pixelsquid
3D Images
pixelsquid.com

iStockphoto
Getty's Microstock Image Site
istockphoto.com

Shutterstock
Another Microstock Site
shutterstock.com

Stockfresh
Cheap Microstock Site
stockfresh.com

VectorStock
Vectors and Illustrations with Some Free Images
vectorstock.com

Free Sites

Death to the Stock Photo
Photos Sent Via Email
deathtothestockphoto.com

FindA.Photo
Photo Site with Handy Color Search
finda.photo

Life of Vids
Royalty-Free Videos, Clips and Loops
lifeofvids.com

Negative Space
High-Res Photos with No Restrictions
negativespace.co

New Old Stock
Vintage Photos from Public Archives
nos.twnsnd.co

Pexels
Curates Photos from Many Free Sites
pexels.com

Pixabay
Photos, Vectors and Video
pixabay.com

StockSnap
Image Site with Robust Search Engine
stocksnap.io

Unsplash
Curated Photos with Email Subscription
unsplash.com

Videvo
Video Clips and Stock Footage
videvo.net

Also Check Out...

Envato Marketplace
Low-Priced Images, Templates, Audio and Tons of Stuff
envato.com

Envato is a collection of freelance design sites that allow you to buy royalty-free everything, from audio clips to images to PowerPoint designs to every electronic template you might ever need. I have purchased templates for websites, presentations and printed material, as well as little add-ons for WordPress (Page 182) and more.

Hot Topic:
Getty Images

With everyone in the world stealing **Getty Images** (gettyimages.com) from the web, the company gave up the fight somewhat. Getty now lets you embed many of its images on your site using its code—for free!

Create Flyers, Social Media Posts and Other Graphics

If you don't have an excellent graphic designer on call, and if you're graphically challenged yourself, here are tools that help you fake it.

Start with...

Canva

Design Templates for Instant Social
   Media Posts, Flyers, Invitations and Much More

canva.com

Non-artistic folks like me need templates and simple instructions to create professional-looking graphics, and **Canva** is just the thing. The site provides frameworks for everything from Facebook timeline images to presentation slides to business cards. It takes just a few minutes to make a badge, invitation or poster with a few clicks of the mouse—perfect for small-business folks who just need a quick graphic for a newsletter, social media post or website.

Canva is free to use for individuals. If you're working with a design team with branding guidelines, you can sign up for Canva for Work for about $10 per user per month. This gives your design team the ability to set color schemes, make their own templates, resize any graphic with a click and more. The service also makes money selling high-quality backgrounds and images for your graphics for a buck each. The images it sells are generally cheaper than you'll pay buying the graphics yourself directly from the original source. If you use your own images, you pay nothing extra.

Canva is another favorite of the NerdHerd. Loyda Villarreal from SA SCUBA Shack says, "Canva is super easy to create quality graphic flyers, posters, social media posts or headers using existing templates or creating my own." And Cheryl Bowie adds, "Since I'm not too artistic, it took a minute for me to get used to using Canva. Now it is my go-to tool for adding text to photos, creating ads and making business cards."

Then Try...

Adobe Spark Post

Design Templates with
  Animation for Instant Social
  Media Posts
spark.adobe.com

Crystal Washington in Adobe Spark Post

Like Canva, **Adobe Spark Post** lets you quickly create beautiful graphics and videos for social media and marketing. With dozens and dozens of templates, you can write a few words, choose a pic, apply a theme and share. Apple device owners can download the app, and everyone can use the tool online.

Three things make Adobe Spark Post cooler than Canva:

- You can animate the text on your graphic to make your post stand out. Canva makes you pay for that feature.
- After you design a graphic, you can easily and quickly transform the image to a number of shapes, both custom and pre-set for social media.
- Adobe Spark Post is actually one of a suite of cool tools Adobe has released under the umbrella of Adobe Spark. The other tools help you create presentations, videos (Page 234) and web pages.

PosterMyWall

Flyer and Sign Templates
postermywall.com

Teachers turned me on to **PosterMyWall**, which specializes in templates for quick signs and flyers. With categories such as fundraising, job fair, women's day and science fair (for starters), the templates cover almost any scenario of a poster you might need.

DESIGN

Also Check Out...

WordSwag

Text-Over-Image App

wordswag.co

Oh my goodness but I love **WordSwag**! It's one of my favorite on-the-go tools to add a little somethin'-somethin' to my social media posts. The thing that makes this tool so cool is that the text comes in formatted, and you don't have to have an eye for design to create a fancy quote.

I'm not the only one who loves WordSwag. NerdHerder Alyssa Godfrey says, "The app is great for creating quotables for social posts. It can be done on a mobile device and then used across your many social media accounts. It's a great way to dress up some text on-the-go." And Phil Gerbyshak, a fellow nerdy speaker, adds...

Lisa Braithwaite in WordSwag

> I look super cool whenever I take a picture at an event and share something smart someone said using WordSwag. It literally takes me 60 seconds... and it's perfectly sized, it looks cool, and it's something people share everywhere.
>
> P.S.—I can add my logo to it if I save it as a transparent .PNG file.
>
> P.P.S.—I am not a designer AT ALL, but my designer friends love it, too—and they can make me a transparent .PNG of my logo because I don't know how to do that!

Create Infographics

• •

Infographics take on the job of converting big data into understandable ideas, and they're all the rage on social media. Use these template-based infographic tools to make some of your own.

Easel.ly

Easy-to-Use Infographic Templates
easel.ly

The easiest infographic tool award goes to **Easel.ly**. Just open a template and start changing the words, colors and layout.

How easy is it? Just ask NerdHerder Cheryl Paglia. "This was so easy to use—I created an account, logged in, and in a matter of minutes was on my way to creating a really beautiful infographic—which I used as a retractable banner for our big trade show. Like falling off a log."

The upgrade is just $36 a year… worth it if you need the extra templates and options.

Piktochart

Infographic Templates with Flexible Data Points
piktochart.com

Although the templates in **Piktochart** can be a little hard to work with, this tool is best for visually representing your data. The charts and graphs are dynamic parts of the infographic, and they can be updated automatically through a connection to Google Sheets. You can choose from a large number of graph styles, including pictographs, histograms and the ever-popular pie charts.

Also Check Out...

Google Sheets   #NerdPartyTrick
Google's Spreadsheet Tool with Magic Analysis Buttons
google.com/drive

Google Sheets has gotten awesome. The somewhat-boring spreadsheet app from Google now has a secret strength that will make you forget that you never took an Excel class.

We all know spreadsheets can help you analyze data in all kinds of ways, but if you're like me, you struggle with formulas. I can't tell you the number of times I've tried to get the data to reveal its secrets and ended up just counting lines with my finger on the screen.

But now Google Sheets has a little button in the bottom right corner of the sheet: Explore. When you click on the button, a pop-up window analyzes the data in your sheet and guesses what kinds of information you might be looking for. Ask it a question, and the Explore feature will answer. If you're interested (which I'm not), it'll reveal the formula that it used to pull the info. You can also highlight certain columns or rows to get specific data points. Super helpful. Also, the charts and data you're offered depend on the type of data you're using. Again, I say… #omg!

Bonus Spreadsheet Tool: Airtable

Airtable
Spreadsheet Tool with Database Capabilities
airtable.com

If you're using a spreadsheet to manage inventory, layers of data or larger projects, it might be time to upgrade to **Airtable**. This tool adds layers of organizational tools to spreadsheets to help you do what Excel wizards can do: group, sort, pivot, link, reference, filter… the advanced capabilities go on and on.

Create GIFs

GIF stands for Graphics Interchange Format, and Wikipedia says it was introduced by CompuServe in 1987. Although many people pronounce it like the word "gift" without the "t," it's supposed to rhyme with the peanut butter named Jif, as in "Choosy programmers choose GIF."

An animated GIF is basically a series of pictures with a teeny tiny time delay between them. Animated GIFs are the little movies we're seeing all over the web. When we use them in social media and online, we can embed others' GIFs or create our own.

Start with...

Giphy and Giphy Cam
Giphy's Mobile Apps
giphy.com/apps

Giphy just keeps coming up with new and easier ways to find and create GIFs. I use Giphy every week for GIFs for my NerdWords newsletter. The site is easy to search, and you can create GIFs from YouTube videos or your own multimedia or pictures.

Giphy's apps take GIFs to new levels. You can add GIFs to your messages right through your keyboard with **Giphy Keys**. Using **Giphy Cam** you can create your own GIFs with special effects and fun filters. And **Giphy Stickers** helps you find, make and share animated stickers, because like middle school, stickers are still a thing.

Then Try...

MomentCam
GIF and Emoji App for Your Selfies
momentcamofficial.com

MomentCam lets you turn your face (or a colleague's) into a little cartoon GIF or emoji that you can share in messages and on social media. They're fun to add to emails as well, since many email systems support GIFs. They're fun, fast and very expressive.

D.J. Rausa in MomentCam

Also Check Out...

If you look beyond their adorableness and the childlike "wow" factor, you should be able to figure out how to make use of these fun apps at work.

Bitmoji

Personalized Emoji App

bitmoji.com

Phil Gerbyshak in Bitmoji

Perhaps the release of **Bitmoji** was the tipping point for our universal obsession with emojis. The tool lets you create a personalized character that can be transformed into hundreds of little emojis. These can be great for showing your enthusiasm for your colleagues' new presentation.

Ditty

Musical App to Turn Any Phrase into a Song

ditty.co

This is pure #NerdJoy. **Ditty** enables you to take any 50-character phrase and make it musical. With just a few clicks, you can make your tagline sing… literally. Or add a dramatic flair to an upcoming deadline. Or impress your nephews. Or whatever. Download the free app, add a phrase and choose a song. Some songs are free, but you can purchase others individually for a buck or so.

Pixton

Cartoons and Comic Strips

pixton.com

If you need a little cartoon of yourself or want to start a comic strip, check out **Pixton**. I love that you can create a character then click buttons to change the person's position without having to redraw.

Design a Logo

••

Your logo is a representation of your brand and a hugely important piece of the puzzle when you create your company's identity. Professionally designed logos take time, money and patience, plus lots of expertise from experienced and smart designers.

But sometimes you just don't have the money or the time. That's where online logo design services can come in handy.

Start with...

Logojoy
AI-Based Logo Tool
logojoy.com

If you're short on time and need a simple logo, **Logojoy** might be the answer. The site uses artificial intelligence to meld the design elements you seek into reality. After filling out a couple of questions, you pick favorites from the generated options. Every time you show a preference, Logojoy evaluates your input to generate more ideas that you might like more.

After you decide on a logo, you pay $65 to buy everything you need to use your new logo.

Tailor Brands
Online DIY Logo Design
tailorbrands.com

Withoomph
Online DIY Logo Design
withoomph.com

Both **Tailor Brands** and **Withoomph** start with wizards to help guide you through the logo-making process. Tailor divides the logo types into three categories: icon-based, name-based and initial-based. Then the system presents a bunch of type styles and asks you to choose which style you like. Tailor then generates six designs for your review, placing them artfully on business cards, websites, shopping bags, t-shirts… all the places your logo might show up. Choose a basic logo, and then fine tune everything from the colors to the fonts and more.

Withoomph is a lot faster and offers many more logo ideas, though the ones it generated for me were laughable. No matter which logo builder you try, you can pay their low fees to get the graphics that you can start using right away… or you can just use them for inspiration and keep designing your own logo.

Also Check Out...

99designs
Crowdsourced Design Contests
99designs.com

Let's say your organization has a big event every year, and you're looking for a logo that would brand the conference series. You could hire your favorite graphic designer to come up with 10 to 20 ideas for several hundred to several thousand dollars. Or you could hold a logo design contest on a crowdsourcing site like **99designs** for $299+ to have dozens of designers come up with ideas that you could narrow down to your top choices and share with your potential attendees for a vote.

DESIGN

I adore these kinds of contests, both for finding the perfect logo and for strengthening your community. Rather than getting one expert's ideas for your logo, you get ideas from many. I had more than 100 variations of my present logo before I picked the best one. As the contest continues, you can give feedback to your top contenders to get them to refine and rework the colors and designs to help bring your vision to life. 99designs also helps you find designers for book covers, T-shirt designs and much more.

Quick Reference Guide

QUICK REFERENCE

Collaborate 33

• •

Collaborate on Files 34

Google Drive 34
Real-Time Collaboration in a Robust Office Suite
google.com/drive

Microsoft Office 365 34
Office Suite with Collaboration Features
microsoft.com/office365

Folia 35
Clean File-Sharing Site for Feedback from Teams
folia.com

GoToMyPC 35
Remote Access Tool
gotomypc.com

Share Large Files 36

WeTransfer 36
Easy File-Sharing Service
wetransfer.com

DropSend 36
Classic File-Sharing Tool
dropsend.com

MediaFire 36
File-Sharing Service for Media Files
mediafire.com

Balloon 37
File Sharing for Dropbox
balloon.io

Bitly 37
URL-Shortener
bitly.com

Manage Projects 38

Trello 38
Project Management Tool Good for Personal Task Management
trello.com

Asana 39
Favorite Project Management Tool with Robust Free Version
asana.com

Smartsheet 39
Spreadsheet-Based Project Management Tool
smartsheet.com

Basecamp 39
Classic Project Management System
basecamp.com

Freedcamp 40
(Almost) Free Project Management System
freedcamp.com

Podio 40
Customizable Project Management System
podio.com

Meet Virtually 41

Cisco Spark 41
Online Meeting Tools with Meeting Management
ciscospark.com

FaceTime 41
Apple's Videoconferencing Tool
apple.com/facetime

Communicate 45

QUICK REFERENCE

Learn a New Language   86

Duolingo   86
Gamified Free Language-Learning
  System
duolingo.com

Tandem   86
Language Practice App
tandem.net

ELSA   87
English Pronunciation Assistance
elsanow.io

Use Study Aids   88

Photomath   88
App that Solves Math Problems
  with a Click
photomath.net

Anki   88
Flashcards to Study Wherever
  You Go
ankisrs.net

Cram   88
Another Flashcard App
cram.com

TinyCards   88
Duolingo Flashcard App
tinycards.duolingo.com

Primer   89
Quick Sales and Marketing Training
yourprimer.com

Justia   89
Law Research Site
law.justia.com/cases

Check the Weather   90

Dark Sky   90
Unnervingly Precise Weather App
darksky.net

What the Forecast?!!   90
Weather Forecasts with Giggles
nightcatproductions.com/
  whattheforecast

Weather Underground   90
Best Overall Weather App
wunderground.com

WunderMap   91
Online Weather Tracker from
  Weather Underground
wunderground.com/wundermap

Storm   91
Weather Underground's
  Storm-Tracking App
wunderground.com/storm

Improve My Writing   92

Hemingway App   92
Online Writing Editor
hemingwayapp.com

PaperRater   93
Online Writing Editor with Option for
  Paper Submissions
paperrater.com

Ginger Page   93
Writing Help for Your Mobile Device
gingersoftware.com

Grammarly   93
English Teacher on Your Laptop
grammarly.com

Organize Citations for Online Research 94

Mendeley   94
Research and Bibliography Tool
  with Mobile Apps
mendeley.com

Zotero   94
Research and Bibliography Tool
zotero.com

PaperShip   95
iOS App for Mendeley and Zotero
papershipapp.com

Discover New Apps and Tools 96

Product Hunt   96
The Ultimate Source for New
  Technology
producthunt.com

AppAdvice Apps Gone Free   96
Best iOS Apps Gone Free Every Day
appadvice.com/apps-gone-free

AppGratis   96
One Free App Every Day
appgratis.com

Lifehacker   98
lifehacker.com

Mashable   98
mashable.com

TechCrunch   98
techcrunch.com

Kim Komando   98
Tech Tool Guru
komando.com

Utilities 99

Capture Info from Computer Screens 100

Jing and/or **Snagit   100**
The Best Screencapture Tools
techsmith.com

Screencast-O-Matic   101
Browser-Based Screen Recorder
screencastomatic.com

Screencastify   101
Another Browser-Based Screen
  Recorder
screencastify.com

Reflector   101
Screen Mirroring Tool for Your
  Mobile Devices
airsquirrels.com/reflector

Create and Edit PDFs 102

Adobe Reader   102
The Original PDF Tool
get.adobe.com/reader

Foxit Reader   103
Windows Adobe Reader Alternative
foxitsoftware.com/products/
  pdf-reader

Adobe Fill & Sign   103
Adobe's PDF Form Filler
In App Stores

Type More Efficiently 104

Fleksy   104
Custom Mobile Keyboard with
  Super-Smart Predictive Text
fleksy.com

HISTORY Here 145

App to Discover an Area's History

history.com/history-here

Yelp Monacle 145

Location-Based Business Finder with
Reviews

yelp.com

Heads Up 145

Ellen DeGeneres' Award-Winning
Family Game

ellentv.com/page/2013/04/23/
heads-up

RunPee 146

Database App that Shares the Best
Time for a Bathroom Run During
a Movie

runpee.com

SitOrSquat 146

Bathroom Review App Brought to
You by Charmin

sitorsquat.com

Stay Safe on the Go 147

SafeTrek 147

Safety Button that Reaches
Authorities in a Flash

safetrekapp.com

Companion 147

Safety App for a Network of Friends

companionapp.io

EmergenSee 148

Emergency App with Live Video
Streaming

emergensee.com

Nextdoor 148

Social Network for Neighborhoods

nextdoor.com

Last Message 148

Android App that Alerts Friends
of a Low Battery

fat-brain.it

Navigate Smartly 149

Google Maps 149

Worldwide Navigation System
with Real-Time Updates

google.com/maps

Waze 149

Crowdsourced Navigation App
with Real-Time Updates

waze.com

HERE WeGo 151

International Map App with Transit
Options

here.com

CityMaps2Go 151

International City Map App with
Travel Insight

ulmon.com

FlightAware 151

Flight Tracker with Airport Delay Info

flightaware.com

brettapproved 152

Site that Helps People with
Disabilities Travel Easier

brettapproved.com

BringFido 152

Site to Discover Pet-Friendly
Businesses

bringfido.com

Travefy 152

Group Travel Management

travefy.com

QUICK REFERENCE

App Index

LET BETH BE YOUR ATTENDEES' NERDY BEST FRIEND!

Since her first Commodore 64 computer, **Beth Ziesenis** has made a verb out of the word nerd. She's here to help you filter through thousands of apps, gadgets, widgets and doodads to find the perfect free and bargain technology tools and work at home.

Although the only real trophy she ever won was for making perfect French fries at McDonald's in high school, Beth Z has been featured on Best Speaker lists by several meeting professionals' publications. She has written four books on apps and speaks to about 10,000 people a year, about 9,999 of whom can't pronounce her last name.

Hire Beth Z

Beth's attendees leave her sessions saying, "This session was worth the price of my whole conference!" She presents keynotes, breakouts, webinars and workshops to audiences of 10-1000.

To inquire about bringing nerdiness to your attendees and programs, contact Nerd HQ at 619-231-9225 or beth@yournerdybestfriend.com.

Beth Ziesenis
Your Nerdy Best Friend

www.yournerdybestfriend.com